For good friend Shyrle Hacker, author and teacher, who generously took over the teaching of one of my Creative Writing classes so that I could have extra time to complete this book, and to Jackie Walsh, editor, whose expertise has deepened whatever quality this book may have.

PRESSURE COOKING

by
Alma Payne Ralston

Illustrated by Mike Nelson

© Copyright 1977
Nitty Gritty Productions
Concord, California

A Nitty Gritty Book*
Published by
Nitty Gritty Productions
P.O. Box 5457
Concord, California 94524

*Nitty Gritty Books — Trademark
Owned by Nitty Gritty Productions
Concord, California

ISBN 0-911954-43-0
Library of Congress Catalog Card Number: 77-82343

Library of Congress Cataloging in Publication Data

Ralston, Alma Payne.
    Pressure cooking.

    Includes index.
    1. Pressure cookery. I. Title.
TX840.P7R34   641.5'87   77-82343
ISBN 0-911954-43-0

Table of Contents

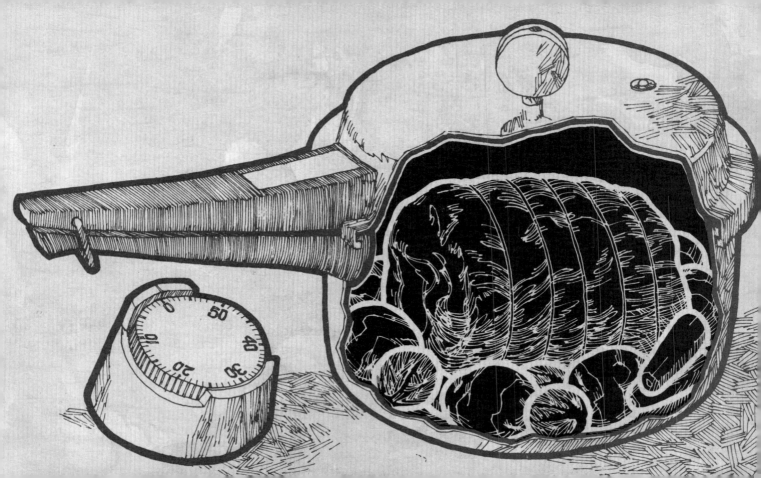

Introduction

Today we are thinking more than ever about how to get the greatest nutrient value from the food we eat. This involves consumer awareness and information about wise food selection, storage for greatest usefulness and preparation of foods so that their nutritional return to the body will be optimal.

Once you have used a pressure cooker, you know what a hard worker it can be. It saves time for the busy career person or homemaker; it saves food and flavor and color, and it saves maximum vitamins and minerals plus cooking fuel—ENERGY—that Number 1 concern of all of us these days—by using fast steam cooking. The result? Tasty foods, whether simple home dishes or fancy ones with a gourmet flair. Just as the microwave oven lends its special magic to baked specialties, the pressure cooker does its special thing for foods that are usually boiled, steamed, stewed or baked.

In regular cooking methods, some of the vitamin content of foods is lost (particularly vitamin C) through oxidation and long cooking. Since pressure cooking is fast cooking and is done in the absence of light and air and with a minimum amount of water and fat, oxidation is eliminated and nutrient loss is minimized.

Of course, pressure cooking can't restore vitamin or mineral loss occasioned by poor selection or long storage before use.

It behooves the shopper to buy only fresh, unblemished fresh fruits, vegetables and meat at their prime if pressure cooking is to operate at its highest level.

Health authorities agree that cooking under pressure gives the most modern, scientific method for mineral and vitamin preservation. This benefit to health . . . the natural way . . . cannot be emphasized too strongly.

Moneywise, this method of cooking not only saves you in fuel cost but also allows you to buy the less expensive cuts of meat and get pleasing results. Shrinkage is also reduced to a minimum.

You'll find as you experiment to get the fullest return from your pressure cooker, that you can do almost anything in the cooker, if you combine it with browning of meats prior to cooking under pressure. Even baby foods, desserts, and canning.

The recipes presented in the various sections have been developed in a 4-quart pressure cooker. For a larger or smaller one, consult your manufacturer's booklet of instruction.

Now go into the kitchen, knowing that you can get that meal onto the table in 10 to 30 minutes. Bon Appetit! And good nutrition too!

Alma Payne Ralston

FROM ANCIENT ODDITY TO MODERN ENERGY SAVER

Talk about being natural and modern, one of our age-old pieces of kitchen equipment is making headlines these days. It is the *pressure cooker*. Long used as the power to turn huge turbines in ocean-going ships, this same kind of power has been confined in a modern saucepan for today's busy cook.

Historically, the idea of cooking by steam may have been accidental. Perhaps early man dropped hot stones into water and saw steam swirl upward. He didn't know what to do with the steam or how to use it. Anyone who has seen the ancient Stonehenge slabs may very well have asked if the men of that time propelled the movement of the mammoth stones by steam. We know that as early as 120 B.C. a writer of Alexandria described a toy made to revolve by steam.

Denis Papin, a young physicist, is the first man whose inventive work led to modern pressure cooking. He invented the first steam piston engine and installed it in a paddlewheel boat. This was powered by a pumping engine and a device for cooking under pressure. He called it a "New Digestor or Engine for Softening Bones." He neatly fitted a deep container with a tight lid to withstand the pressure produced by high temperatures and even devised a safety valve to prevent excessive temperature rise.

Invited to demonstrate his unusual creation, he appeared before the Royal Society in London in 1682. The members—amateurs and scientists—were impressed with his work. But the construction of the device was crude and people were afraid to use it. As with microscopes and other "curiosities" of those days, mankind had to wait for the unraveling of additional scientific facts to apply their scientific discoveries to commercial and home use.

A century and a half later Napoleon announced a prize for a method of supplying his troops with food. (Nicholas) Francois Appert, a French chef, went to work. He revived interest in Papin's work and produced the first successful canning appliance.

In 1917 the U.S. Department of Agriculture announced that the only safe method of canning low-acid foods was under pressure, thus promoting the demand for pressure cookers/canners. But it wasn't until 1938 that the first saucepan-sized cooker was marketed. Years of testing and refinement have given us our present-day, high temperature, low-energy-user, pressure cooker. And for all-around use to preserve the highest amount of nutrient value in natural foods for your health and mine, the pressure cooker has recently nudged its way into a select group of important kitchen aids.

CONSUMER INFORMATION

Pressure cookers come in standard and deluxe models and there are variations in procedures depending upon the model. Reread manufacturer's directions to get maximum results from your cooker.

Pressure cooking makes use of latest technology to cook foods quickly while retaining flavor and nutrient goodness. It depends upon a few simple principles; they are:

1. *Liquid boils rapidly and fills cooker with live steam.* **Water, juice or other liquid must be added to cooker before pressure cooking can commence in order to create this steam. The liquid added to cooker is almost instantly converted into live steam when cooker is placed over high to medium heat. Foods will expand while cooking. This is why you** *never fill cooker* **more than 2/3 to 3/4 full depending upon model and have at least 1-1/4 inches clear space between rim of cooker and contents for expansion to take place without explosion and food on ceiling!**

2. *Lips of gasket spread apart as pressure builds up to create steamtight chamber*

for cooking. Never open cooker until all pressure has been reduced.

3. *Air and steam are forced from cooker through vent on cover.* **Pressure will never fall below selected level as long as sufficient heat is applied to cooker and control jiggles 1 to 4 times a minute. Be sure to lower or raise heat to keep at desired level.**

4. *Live steam under pressure rises above boiling point and penetrates food, cooking it very quickly, yet preserving nutrients, color, juices and texture. Live steam under pressure tenderizes protein foods naturally without addition of chemical additives.*

Steam penetrates food particles from all sides as opposed to food cooked in baths of water. Pressure cooking helps prevent water-soluble B complex and C vitamins, minerals, salts and flavorful sugars from leeching out in cooking. Since pressure cooking is done in absence of air, the oxidative loss of vitamins, such as A and C is lowered, according to the Mirro Aluminum Company. Saves fuel energy too. And it has built-in safety devices against unwanted bacteria because of the high temperature under which food cooks. As liquid in bottom of cooker is converted into steam, air is expelled through vent tube. Weighted pressure control allows pressure to be built up to desired

level. As pressure continues to rise further, the control rises slightly and jiggles. This allows enough steam to escape to keep pressure constant. Pressures will not fall below selected level as long as sufficient heat is applied to cooker and control jiggles 1 to 4 times per minute.

Live steam under pressure raises temperature in cooker above 212°F, which is the highest temperature attainable by boiling water at sea level. *At 5 pounds pressure, internal temperature is 228°F. This temperature is recommended for cooking custards, steamed breads and puddings. It is also recommended for terminal sterilization of baby bottles and formulas.*

At 10 pounds pressure, internal temperature is 240°F, which is recommended for cooking protein foods, such as meat poultry and fish. At this setting you will have less shrinkage of these expensive foods.

At 15 pounds pressure, internal temperature is 250°F, which is recommended for cooking all fresh and frozen vegetables, dried fruits, cereals and soups.

HOW TO USE YOUR PRESSURE COOKER

Although the principle of generating steam for cooking is the same in all pressure cookers, operation of the control or pressure regulator varies slightly from make to make so it is imperative that you follow manufacturer's directions for use. There are safeguards to follow in all pressure cooking. Some of the most important ones are:

1. Use more if you choose, *but never less water than called for* when adapting your own recipes. Always add 1 cup or more liquid to roasts after browning and cover cooker at once to preserve maximum steam.
2. Liquids other than water constitute part of liquid necessary and should be deducted from total liquid called for in any recipe.
3. When you choose to use rack always add 1/4 more liquid than called for.
4. Always reduce heat when regulator (or control) begins to jiggle or rock. It should move 1 to 4 times a minute to produce desired finished product. Use low or medium setting on electric range to maintain this pressure, or simmer on gas range.
5. During the course of steaming if you notice a slight leakage around air vent

or pipe, this is natural. But if this persists, examine automatic air vent to see if food has collected there or if some part of cooker needs to be tightened.

6. Leakage between cover and body suggests sealing ring or gasket is not in place or needs to be replaced.

7. Realize that all cooking times specified can only be approximate. Condition of ingredients used, size of fresh produce varies, pressure of home gas or electricity varies and certain other uncontrollable variations. So know your own cooker and range condition.

8. When adapting your own recipes for dishes that are to be cooked in a mold or casserole covered with double fold of heavy foil be sure to increase cooking time. To secure foil, crimp edges tightly to seal. As an added precaution, tie with string.

9. Two methods for reducing pressure instantly may be used — cooling cooker under cold running water or setting cooker in pan of cold water. The first method is faster.

10. When reducing pressure by placing cooker under cold running water take care not to let water get into cooker through steam vent.

11. When you want to cook 2 or more vegetables at the same time, it is not necessary to place in separate containers as flavors will not mingle.

12. Don't use high heat to bring up pressure when cooking cereals, pastas, rice, dried vegetables or other foods that are apt to froth while cooking. Always add 1 tablespoon oil to counteract froth, and bring pressure up slowly.

13. When you want to drain liquid from cooked food remove gasket from cover, recover and let liquid drain through "apertures."

14. Never substitute oil for required amount of liquid in any recipe.

15. Always consult manufacturer's handbook for specific information about your particular cooker.

Soups Fit For A King And Queen

What better way to begin a lunch or dinner than with soup? And what faster or more excellent way to make it than in a pressure cooker? Soup can be light to tickle taste buds or hearty enough to be a main dish. By adding a green salad and French bread you can have an easy, complete main meal with little effort.

When you use your pressure cooker for soup making *allow at least 1-1/4 inches (or more according to manufacturer's directions) space between rim of cooker and top of liquid. Do not cook LENTIL, PEARL BARLEY OR SPLIT PEA SOUP in cooker unless you follow special procedures* **as they tend to froth and clog vent tube.** *Always add 1 tablespoon oil to water in cooker when preparing frothy soups.*

After removing cooked soup from the heat *check pressure reduction by nudging the control to be sure all steam is expelled before opening cooker.* **You may get a hissing sound without any steam. This is the sound of air entering cooker and does not indicate pressure. If no steam comes out you can safely open cooker. If steam spurts out, pressure is not completely reduced and further cooling is needed.**

Never handle pressure control with hands. **Use a long meat fork or tongs, depending on the design of the control. Observe safety procedures to avoid accidents.**

13

CREAM OF ASPARAGUS CUSTARD SOUP

1/2 can (10-3/4 ozs.) cream of asparagus soup
3/4 cup hot milk (not boiled)
1 tsp. instant minced onion
1/8 tsp (scant) thyme, optional

1/8 tsp. (scant) nutmeg
3 egg yolks, lightly beaten
1 cup water
paprika

In a mixing bowl combine asparagus soup with milk. Stir to blend evenly. Add seasonings and egg yolks. Blend thoroughly. Correct seasonging. Pour into 3 individual aluminum molds or oven proof cups. Cover with a double layer of aluminum foil firmly secured. Place rack in cooker. Add water and set molds on rack. Cover and allow steam to flow from vent to release all air. Set control at 5. Cover and cook 2-1/2 minutes after control jiggles. (For cookers having 15 pound setting only, remove cooker from heat as soon as control jiggles.) Reduce pressure normally. Remove cover and sprinkle each mold with paprika. Tops will be partially set. Serve at once. Makes 3 servings.

Variation

Cream of pea or vegetable soup may be substituted for asparagus soup.

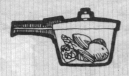

CREAM OF ARTICHOKE SOUP

This is a very delicate cold soup. It is also good served hot!

1 pkg. (9 ozs.) frozen artichoke hearts
3 leeks, sliced thin
1 cup water
1/2 tsp. salt
1/8 tsp. white pepper

1 can (13-1/2 ozs.) chicken broth
1 tsp. lemon juice
1 cup heavy cream
nutmeg
sprigs parsley

Place artichoke hearts and leeks in cooker. Add water, salt and pepper. Cover and set control at 15. Cook 15 minutes after control jiggles. Remove and cool at once under cold running water. Uncover and pour mixture into blender container. Add broth and lemon juice. Blend at high speed about 1 minute. Pour into bowl and slowly blend in cream. Cover and chill. If serving hot, return mixture to cooker and add cream. Warm slowly over lowest heat, stirring constantly. Serve with a dash of nutmeg or garnish each bowl with a sprig of parsley. Makes 6 servings.

CHILLED CAULIFLOWER POTAGE SUPREME

1 cauliflower
1 onion, coarsely chopped
1/2 cup water
6 tbs. margarine
1 tsp. salt
1/4 tsp. white pepper
6 tbs. flour
1 qt. milk
1/2 tsp. horseradish
2 drops Tabasco sauce
1/8 tsp. curry powder
1 cup light cream, optional
whipped cream, optional
minced parsley

Remove outer leaves of cauliflower and cut stem close to head. Break off flowerets, wash and put into cooker. Add onion and water. Cover and set control at 15.

Cook 1 minute after control jiggles. Reduce pressure at once by setting cooker under cold running water. Drain cauliflower and place in mixing bowl. Season with salt and pepper. Melt margarine in cooker and blend in flour. Gradually stir in milk. Simmer gently, stirring constantly until milk thickens. Add cauliflower and cook until very soft. Pour soup mixture into food processor bowl or blender container and purée. Add horseradish, Tabasco and curry. Blend again. Pour into bowl and refrigerate. At serving time, add cream, if a richer soup is wanted, and float a dollop of whipped cream on each serving. Sprinkle with parsley. Makes 5 to 6 servings.

When you are ready to drain vegetables, all you have to do is slip out gasket around cover rim, replace cover without gasket and drain. Food cannot slip because cover is held in place while liquid drains through "apertures."

CREAM OF CUCUMBER SOUP

Cool and refreshing on a hot day, this delicate soup is bound to please.

3 cucumbers
1 small onion
1/4 cup water
2 cans (13-1/2 ozs.) chicken broth
3 tbs. margarine
3 tbs. flour

1 cup hot milk
1/2 tsp. salt
1/8 tsp. white pepper
1/2 cup thin cream
tarragon leaves

Peel and slice cucumbers. Remove seeds from slices. Place in cooker. Slice onion paper thin and add to cooker along with 1/4 cup water. Simmer until tender. Add chicken broth. Cover and set control at 15. Cook 2 minutes after control jiggles. Reduce pressure normally for 5 minutes, then place cooker under cold running water. In small mixing bowl blend margarine and flour. Heat milk in saucepan. Gradually add butter-flour mixture to hot milk, stirring constantly to avoid lumping. Add to cooker. Cook, stirring until cucumber mixture thickens slightly. Remove from heat. Season

with salt & pepper. Cool and stir in cream. Refrigerate until serving time. Serve garnished with fresh tarragon leaves or a sprinkling of tarragon. Makes 6 servings.

Variations

For a richer soup, use whipping cream instead of light cream and top with a dollop of whipped cream.

Paprika sprinkled over the top of this or any cream soup is pretty to the eye and sharpens the flavor.

One to 2 tablespoons dry sherry or vermouth gives a piquant flavor to cream soups.

Never fill cooker with more than 10-2/3 to 12 cups (depending upon brand) of liquid or other ingredients.

POTATO-SPINACH SOUP

1 can (10-3/4 ozs.) potato soup
1 pkg. (8 ozs.) chopped spinach, defrosted
1 can water
1/4 cup dry sherry
1 tsp. instant minced onion
1/8 tsp. nutmeg
Sesame Croutons, page 23

   Pour soup into cooker. Place spinach in food processor bowl or blender container. Add water and purée. Pour into cooker. Add remaining ingredients and blend carefully with soup. Cover and set control at 15. Cook 1-1/2 minutes after control jiggles. Reduce pressure at once under cold running water. Uncover and ladle into individual bowls. Serve with Sesame Croutons. Makes 4 servings.

Variation

   Frozen chopped broccoli may be substituted for spinach.

20

LOUISIANA SHRIMP JAMBALAYA

2 tbs. vegetable oil
1 clove garlic
1 small onion, chopped
1 slice precooked ham, diced
1 cup uncooked rice
1-1/2 tsp. salt
1/8 tsp. white pepper
1/4 tsp. gumbo filé

dash allspice
1/8 tsp. sweet basil
1-1/2 cups water
1 can (16 ozs.) tomatoes
1 can (6 ozs.) sliced mushrooms and liquid
1 lb. deveined shrimp
1 tbs. minced green pepper

Heat oil in cooker. Saute garlic and onion until light brown. Stir in ham and rice. Cook until rice turns golden, adding a little more oil, if needed. Remove garlic. Add seasonings, water, tomatoes and mushrooms. Mix thoroughly to blend. Add shrimp, and sprinkle green pepper over all. Cover and set control at 15. Cook 5 minutes after control jiggles. Reduce pressure at once by placing cooker under cold running water. Remove cover and let stand a few minutes before serving. Makes 6 or more servings.

21

LONG ISLAND CLAM BISQUE

2 ozs. salt pork
1 small onion, chopped
1 clove garlic, finely chopped
1/2 cup chopped celery
1/2 cup chopped green pepper
2 cans (6-1/2 ozs. ea.) minced clams
2 cups chicken broth
1/3 cup minced parsley
1 potato, peeled and diced
2 cups hot, not boiled, milk
    or 1 cup milk and 1 cup cream
1/4 cup dry sherry
1/8 tsp. white pepper
1/8 tsp. thyme
Sesame Croutons, page 23

Cut salt pork in small pieces. Place in cooker and saute' slowly to render. Add

onion, garlic, celery and green pepper. Sauté over medium heat until soft. Drain clams and measure liquid. Add chicken broth to make 3 cups. Pour into cooker and add sautéed vegetables, clams, parsley and potato. Cover and set control at 15. Cook 6 minutes after control jiggles. Reduce pressure normally 5 minutes then set under cold running water. Uncover and stir in milk, sherry, pepper and thyme. Reheat slowly. Serve with Sesame Croutons. Makes 10 servings.

Sesame Croutons

2 tbs. vegetable oil
2 cups bread, cubed after crusts have been trimmed off
1-1/2 tbs. sesame seed

1/4 tsp. celery salt
salt

Heat oil in cooker or heavy skillet. Add bread cubes and stir so that light browning occurs on all sides. Add sesame seed and celery salt. Continue to cook and stir 1 minute until all bread cubes are coated and sesame seed have turned golden. Turn onto a paper towel. Sprinkle lightly with salt. Cool and store in covered container.

# FISH CHOWDER

Use halibut, sole, turbot or any white fish and you will have a flavorsome, high protein starter for lunch or dinner.

1 lb. fresh or frozen white fish
1 qt. boiling water
1 tsp. salt
1/8 tsp. freshly ground pepper
1 bay leaf
1/2 cup chopped onions

1/2 cup diced celery
1 cup peeled diced potatoes
4 whole cloves
1/4 cup white table wine
1/2 cup cream, optional

Place fish in cooker with boiling water. Cover and set control at 15. Cook 5 minutes after control jiggles. Reduce pressure normally for 5 minutes, then place under cold running water. Uncover. Flake fish and return to cooker. Add remaining ingredients except wine and cream. Cover and set control at 15. Cook 7 minutes after control jiggles. Let cool normally 5 minutes then place cooker under cold running water. Remove cover, lift out bay leaf and stir in wine and cream. Serve at once with a sprinkling of paprika. Makes 6 to 8 servings.

BOUILLABAISSE

Authentically bouillabaisse is concocted in France from fish native to the Mediterranean. But we make very good bouillabaisse from our fish, and here is one recipe that is sure to please.

1/2 lb. haddock or sea bass
1/2 lb. red snapper
1/2 lb. eel, optional
1 small lobster, parboiled
3 tbs. olive oil or margarine
1 onion, chopped
1 leek, cut up
1 small clove garlic

1 tomato, peeled and chopped
bouquet garni (thyme, rosemary,
    bay leaf, parsley and celery)
water
1/8 tsp. (scant) saffron
1-1/2 tsp. salt
1/2 tsp. freshly ground pepper
garlic flavored croutons

Cut fish and lobster into small serving pieces. Heat oil in cooker. Add vegetables and cook 2 minutes. Add bouquet garni (tied in a bag), fish, except lobster, and water to cover. Cover and set control at 15. Cook 5 minutes after control jiggles. Reduce pressure normally for 5 minutes, then place under cold running water. Uncover and

add lobster, saffron, salt and pepper. Reheat and correct seasoning. Remove bouquet garni. Pour soup into warm tureen and serve at table. Place croutons in bottom of each bowl and ladle soup over them. Makes 4 generous servings.

Variations

Add 2 tablespoons sherry or gin for an absolutely unauthentic but delicious flavor enhancer.

Add 1 large potato, cut up, to cooker along with other vegetables. Increase cooking time 6 to 8 minutes.

Add 4 to 8 mussels after other ingredients are cooked and let simmer over low heat until they open.

A variation on garlic flavored croutons would be slices of French bread buttered, rubbed with a clove of garlic and toasted. Ladle soup over them.

When making soup do not fill cooker more than 2/3 to 3/4 full depending upon manufacturer's directions.

MEAT-VEGETABLE SOUP

1-1/2 lbs. soup meat and bone (cracked)
1 onion, thinly sliced
1 tsp. salt
1/8 tsp. freshly ground pepper
4 cups water
1 cup diced potatoes
1/2 cup thinly sliced carrots
1 cup cut green beans

1 stalk celery, diced
1 cup chopped fresh spinach
   or 1 pkg. (10 ozs.) frozen
   chopped spinach
1 cup canned tomatoes
   or 2 medium fresh ones, quartered
3 tbs. finely minced parsley

Place soup meat and bone, onion, salt, pepper and water in cooker. Cover and set control at 15. Cook 50 minutes after control jiggles. Reduce pressure normally for 5 minutes, then place cooker under cold running water. Open cooker and remove bone and meat. Strain broth and cut meat into small pieces. Return to cooker and add vegetables. Cover and set control at 15. Cook for 10 minutes after control jiggles. Cool cooker normally for 5 minutes, then place under cold running water. Correct seasoning. Serve soup from a heated tureen. Garnish with parsley. Makes 8 to 10 servings.

OXTAIL SOUP

1 (about 1-1/2 lbs.) oxtail
1 tsp. salt
1/2 tsp. freshly ground pepper
3 tbs. flour
3 tbs. vegetable oil
1-1/2 qts. water
1/2 cup diced carrot

1/2 cup diced white turnips
1/2 cup diced onion
1/2 cup diced celery
1 tsp. Worcestershire sauce, optional
2 tbs. Madeira or sweet table wine
French bread

Have oxtail cut in 2 inch lengths. Wipe with damp cloth. Sprinkle oxtail with salt, pepper and flour. Heat oil in cooker. Brown oxtail on all sides. Add water. Cover and set control at 15. Cook 50 minutes after control jiggles. Reduce pressure normally 5 minutes, then place under cold running water. Uncover and remove meat and bones. Shred meat and return to cooker. Discard bones. Add remaining ingredients except wine and bread. Cover and set control at 15. Let cook 3 minutes after control jiggles. Reduce pressure normally 5 minutes, then place under cold running water. Add wine and serve with toasted rounds of baguette-type French bread. Makes 10 servings.

FAR EASTERN LENTIL SOUP

This highly seasoned, high protein soup may be made without the ham hock for a vegetarian specialty. And if you do not like zesty seasonings, Indian fashion, omit the coriander, cumin and turmeric.

1 cup lentils
1 qt. water
1 ham hock (1 lb.) cracked
1 tbs. vegetable oil
1/2 cup celery, diced
1/2 cup carrots, diced
1/2 cup onion, thinly sliced

1 tsp. cumin
1 tsp. ground turmeric
1 garlic clove
2 tsp. sugar
1/2 tsp. salt
1/4 tsp. pepper
1 tbs. coriander or parsley

Pour lentils into cooker and cover with water. Let stand overnight. Drain and return lentils to cooker. Add 1 quart fresh water, ham hock and oil. Cover and set control at 15. Cook 30 minutes after control jiggles. Reduce pressure normally 5 minutes, then place cooker under cold running water. Uncover cooker and remove ham hock. Purée lentils and broth with blender, food processor or food mill. Add water to make 3

cups liquid. Return to cooker. Cut ham into cubes. Return to cooker. Add remaining ingredients. Cover and set control at 15. Cook 5 minutes after control jiggles. Reduce pressure at once under cold running water. Uncover and serve hot. Pass a small dish of chopped peanuts and coriander as desired. Makes 6 servings.

Add 1 tablespoon oil to water when cooking foods such as lentils, dry beans, cereals and pastas which tend to froth and might clog the vent.

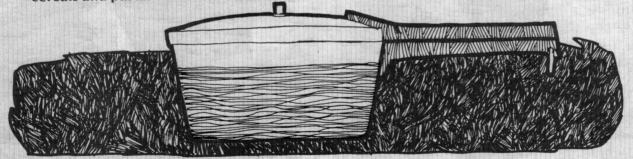

POLISH BORSCH

You may use short ribs, shin bones or any bones with meat to make a base for this delicious winter borsch. I developed this recipe after enjoying a similar one at the Neva Banks Restaurant in Leningrad.

1-1/2 lbs. soup meat and bone
1 qt. water
1 tsp. salt
1/8 tsp. pepper
2 medium onions, thinly sliced
1/2 cup chopped celery
2 cups grated cooked or canned beets
1 cup grated peeled carrots
1 cup shredded cabbage
1/2 cup minced green pepper

1 small bay leaf
1-1/2 tsp. salt
1 can (6 ozs.) tomato paste
2 tbs. vinegar
1 tbs. sugar
1 cup grated potatoes (optional)
1 tsp. dill weed
1 cup sour cream
paprika

Combine meat and bone, water, salt and pepper. Cover and set control at 15. Cook 50 minutes after control jiggles. Reduce pressure normally 5 minutes, then place

cooker under cold running water. Remove bone and meat. Strain and measure broth. Add water if needed to make 1 quart liquid. Shred meat and add to liquid. Add remaining ingredients except sour cream and paprika. Cover and set control at 15. Cook 3 minutes after control jiggles. Cool normally for 5 minutes, then place cooker under cold running water. Serve immediately. Garnish with generous dollops of sour cream and sprinkle with paprika. Makes 10 to 12 servings.

Recipes in this book are constructed for 4-quart cooker so do not overload. Follow manufacturer's directions and do not fill cooker more than stated amount.

RUSSIAN CABBAGE SOUP

I tried to bring home at least one authentic recipe for this soup and was fortunate in finding one in Estonia where it is served as frequently as borsch is in Russia. It should have hard rolls or black bread as an accompaniment to be authentic.

1/4 cabbage, cut in wedges
1 cup sauerkraut
1 qt. soup stock
    or 2 cans (13-3/4 ozs. ea.) chicken broth
1/2 tsp. salt
3 eggs

1 cup rich milk
1/2 cup cold water
3 tbs. margarine
3 tbs. flour
1 flowerette fresh dill
    or 1/2 tsp. dry dill

Place cabbage in cooker. Add sauerkraut and stock. Cover. Set control at 15. Cook for 3 minutes after control jiggles. Remove from heat, and reduce pressure normally 5 minutes, then place cooker under cold running water. Remove cover. Leave vegetables in liquid. Add salt. Beat eggs and mix in milk and water. Add to cooker. Melt margarine and stir in flour to make a paste. Add a few spoonfuls of hot stock, stirring constantly to blend without lumping. Stir in dill. Return to cooker. Stir over low heat until soup

thickens. Correct seasoning. Makes 6 generous servings.

Variations

Soup may be served without thickening as desired.
Experiment with anise or mustard instead of dill for flavor accents.
For a Greek variety, use a leg of lamb bone along with soup stock when cooking the cabbage. Omit eggs and milk; instead use 2 tart apples, chopped and 2 cups chopped tomatoes. Season with 1/4 cup lemon juice, then taste and correct seasonings.

SWEET-SOUR CABBAGE SOUP

This is another of my Russian recipes, this one being adapted from a marvelous soup I had at Hotel Rossya restaurant in Moscow where I tried to get the recipe. No luck. So I concocted this recipe from the flavors I remember of this potage-type soup.

1 can (1 lb.) sauerkraut
1 can (1 lb.) stewed tomatoes
1 can (8 ozs.) tomato sauce
1/4 cup brown sugar
1 tbs. lemon juice
1 unpeeled apple, grated
1 peeled carrot, grated
1/3 cup seedless raisins

1/2 lb. lean ground chuck
1 egg, lightly beaten
1/4 cup cooked rice
1/3 tsp. sweet basil
1/4 tsp. salt
1 tbs. vegetable oil
water
1 bouillon cube

Drain sauerkraut and tomatoes, reserving liquid from both. Combine sauerkraut, tomatoes, tomato sauce, brown sugar, lemon juice, apple, carrot and the raisins in a large bowl. Transfer to cooker. Mix meat with egg, rice, sweet basil and salt. Shape into

1-inch balls. Brown lightly in oil. Place on top of sauerkraut mixture. Measure reserved liquids and add water to make 4 cups. Add to cooker along with bouillon cube. Cover and set control at 15. Cook 15 minutes after control jiggles. Reduce pressure at once under cold running water. Uncover and correct seasoning. Ladle into individual bowls or serve from a tureen at the table. Makes 10 to 12 servings.

Meat — Hearty And Party Fare

A bonanza for the busy homemaker because you can forget all about tenderizing the less tender cut of meat. Pressure cooking tenderizes as it cooks, and at the same time conserves a fourth to a third energy in comparison with amount of energy used by the more conventional methods of cooking. Nutritionally speaking, you can be assured of nutrient conservation, too, and the flavor of the cooked product seems to be rich and full-bodied, just as you like it.

1. Most meats, but not corned beef and tongue, should be browned thoroughly in hot fat or oil (I use the latter for its polyunsaturated content).
2. Give a browning glow to roasts by placing under broiler for 2 to 3 minutes after cooking is completed.
3. Use rack only as directed.
4. Use amount of water indicated even if you adapt your own recipes. Never use less liquid than indicated. If uncertain, use slightly more than is called for.
5. Never overload cooker. See manufacturer's directions on amount to use. Usually this will be not more than 2/3 to 3/4 full so that there is ample space above food and liquid levels for air circulation and expansion.
6. Chicken may rise a little higher in cooker as long as no part of it obstructs

vent tube. Consult manufacturer's directions.

7. When you adapt your own recipes which contain soup stock, vegetable juice or wine, subtract the amount of this liquid from amount of water specified.

8. Do not use milk in meat dishes as it has a tendency to scorch and boil over.

9. Check pressure cooking time and amount of liquid in your manufacturer's handbook when adapting recipes. The cooking time of meats does vary, depending upon cut, grade, amount of bone and other factors, *so time given in recipes is approximate.*

Meats For Pressure Cooking

Beef:
Blade roast
Chuck roast
Corned Beef
Flank Steak
Heart
Liver
Ox tail
Swiss Steak
Rump roast
Shanks
Short Ribs
Stew
Tongue

Pork:
Chops
Heart
Hocks
Shoulder
Steak
Salt Pork
Lamb:
Breast
Heart
Neck
Riblets
Shanks
Shoulder
Stew

Veal:
Breast
Heart
Riblets
Round Steak
Rump
Shanks
Shoulder
Stew
Tongue

SAUCY MEAT BALLS

Zesty Tomato Sauce, page 43
1 lb. ground lean pork
1/4 lb. ground lean beef
1-1/2 cups bread crumbs
1/4 cup milk
2 eggs, lightly beaten
2 tbs. minced onion
1 clove garlic, minced

1/2 cup minced parsley
1/2 cup grated cheddar cheese
1 tsp. salt
1/2 tsp. pepper
1/2 tsp. oregano
2 tbs. oil
3/4 cup water

Prepare sauce as directed. Combine remaining ingredients, except oil and water in large mixing bowl. Form into 2-inch balls, pressing gently. Heat oil in cooker and brown meat balls. Remove from cooker. Add rack and water. Place meat balls on rack. Cover and set control at 10 and cook 5 minutes after control jiggles. (For cookers having 15 pound setting only, decrease cooking time 1 minute.) Reduce pressure normally 5 minutes, then place cooker under cold running water. Uncover and remove rack. Pour sauce over meat balls. Simmer gently 1 hour so that flavor can permeate all. Makes 6 servings.

Zesty Tomato Sauce

1 small onion, chopped fine
1 clove garlic, minced
1/3 tsp. Tabasco sauce
1 large can (1 lb. 13 ozs.) tomato juice
2 tbs. flour

1 tsp. salt
1/4 tsp. black pepper
1 tsp. Worcestershire sauce
1/2 tsp. oregano, crumbled
1/4 tsp. mustard

Blend all together in a heavy saucepan or pressure cooker. Simmer uncovered 45 minutes. Makes 3 cups.

Variations

Let your imagination have a field day in seasoning meat balls. Instead of bread-crumbs, substitute crumbled shredded wheat. And if garlic is not high on your seasoning list, use 1/8 teaspoon allspice or nutmeg. With these flavors, serve a simple meat gravy, with or without mushrooms.

SPEEDY MEAT BALLS

Begin with good, lean beef and use this recipe with any of your favorite variations.

1 lb. ground lean beef
1 cup crumbled French bread
1 egg or egg substitute
1/2 cup nonfat milk
2 tbs. minced onion
1 tsp. salt

1/8 tsp. freshly ground pepper
1/8 tsp. allspice
2 tbs. vegetable oil
1/2 cup water
1/4 cup red table wine

Combine meat, crumbs, egg, milk, onion, salt, pepper and allspice. Blend thoroughly. Form into balls, 1-1/2 inches in diameter. Heat oil in cooker and brown meat balls until golden and a little crusty in appearance. Slip rack under meat balls. Add water and wine. Cover and set control at 10. Cook for 5 minutes after control jiggles. (For cookers having 15 pound setting only, decrease cooking time 1 minute.) Reduce pressure normally for 5 minutes, then place cooker under cold running water. Remove meat balls to hot platter and thicken gravy (See page 53). Pour gravy over meat balls. Serve with hot noodles, baked potatoes or fluffy rice. Makes 4 servings.

MEXICAN HAMBURGERS

1 can (10-3/4 ozs.) tomato soup
1/2 tsp. Worcestershire sauce
1/4 cup catsup
1/2 tsp. salt
1/8 tsp. freshly ground pepper
1 tsp. ground mustard
1/4 tsp. garlic salt
1/2 cup water

1 lb. lean ground beef
1 egg, slighty beaten
1 tbs. green pepper
1 tbs. finely chopped onion
1/2 tsp. salt
2 tbs. margarine
3/4 cup water
4 hamburger buns

Combine soup, Worcestershire, catsup, salt, pepper, mustard, garlic salt and water in saucepan. Simmer at least 30 minutes or as long as an hour to blend flavors. Combine meat, egg, green pepper, onion and salt. Form into 4 patties. Melt margarine in cooker. Brown patties. Slip rack under patties and add water. Cover and set control at 10. Cook 5 minutes after control jiggles. (For cookers having 15 pound setting only, decrease cooking time 2 minutes.) Reduce pressure normally 5 minutes, then place cooker under cold running water to complete. Serve patties on toasted, buttered buns. Top with sauce. Makes 4 servings.

45

SPAGHETTI SAUCE

Add or substract ingredients to make your own flavorsome sauce for pastas.

1/3 cup vegetable oil
1 lb. ground lean beef
1 cup finely minced onion
1/2 tsp. salt
1/2 cup diced green pepper
1/4 cup diced sweet red pepper

1/2 cup sliced mushrooms
1 can (6 ozs.) tomato paste
1 can (1 lb. 4 ozs.) tomatoes
1/4 tsp. oregano
1/8 tsp. sweet basil
freshly ground pepper

Heat oil in cooker and brown meat, stirring as it cooks. Add remaining ingredients. Cover and set control at 10. Cook 5 minutes after control jiggles. (For cookers having 15 pound setting only, decrease cooking time 4 minutes.) Reduce pressure at once by placing cooker under cold, running water. If a thicker sauce is desired, cook uncovered a few minutes. Serve with cooked pasta and sprinkle with grated Romano cheese. Makes 4 servings.

Note: Garlic may be added to seasonings as desired:

46

CHINESE PEPPER STEAK

2 green peppers
1 lb. top round steak
3 tbs. soy sauce

1 tbs. sherry
1/2 tsp. sugar
2 tbs. vegetable oil

1/2 tsp. salt
3/4 cup water
3 tbs. cornstarch

Cut peppers in strips. Set aside. Trim visible fat from meat and cut in strips 1/2 by 4 inches. In large mixing bowl combine 1 tablespoon soy sauce, sherry and sugar. Add meat and toss as you would green salad. Let stand 15 minutes. Toss again. Heat oil in cooker and brown meat. Sprinkle with salt. Add 1/2 cup water. Cover and set control at 10. Cook 7 minutes (10 for pork) after control jiggles. (For cookers having 15 pound setting only, decrease cooking time 2 minutes.) Reduce pressure normally 5 minutes, then place cooker under cold running water. Open cooker and add peppers. Cover and set control at 15. Cook 3 minutes after control jiggles. Reduce pressure at once under cold running water. Remove meat and peppers to warm platter and keep warm. Make a paste of remaining 2 tablespoons cornstarch and 1/4 cup water. Heat to thicken in small saucepan. Stir into hot liquid in cooker. Cook, stirring over medium heat until thickened. Correct seasoning. Spoon over meat and peppers. Serve with hot rice and bean sprouts or a blend of stir-fry vegetables. Pass the soy sauce! Makes 4 servings.

SWISS STEAK WITH VEGETABLES

1/4 cup flour
3/4 tsp. salt
1/8 tsp. pepper
1-1/2 lbs. beefsteak
    (rump, round or chuck)
2-1/2 tbs. vegetable oil

1/2 cup water
1/4 cup onion, chopped
1-1/4 cups stewed tomatoes
1/3 cup celery, diced
1/3 cup sliced carrots

Combine flour, salt and pepper. Cut steak into serving size pieces and dredge in seasoned flour. Pound into steak on both sides as much more flour mixture as it will hold. Heat oil in cooker. Brown steak on all sides until nut brown. Add water. Cover cooker and set control at 10. Cook 25 minutes after control jiggles. (For cookers having 15 pound setting only, decrease cooking time 2 minutes.) Reduce pressure normally 5 minutes, then place cooker under cold running water. Uncover and add remaining ingredients. Set control at 15 and cook 6 minutes after control jiggles. Cool at once by placing cooker under cold running water. Remove meat to warm platter. Pour pan juices over meat, or make gravy (page 53). Makes 5 to 6 servings.

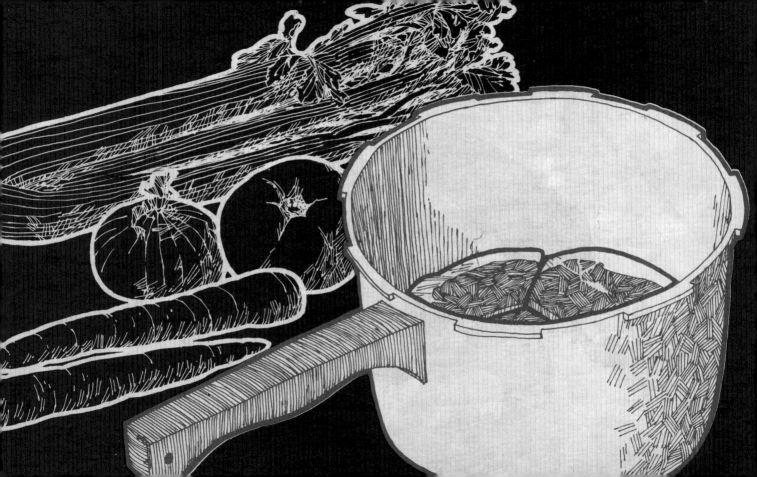

FLANK STEAK WITH PRUNE DRESSING

1 (about 2 lbs.) flank steak
1/2 tsp. salt
1/4 tsp. freshly ground pepper
2 tbs. margarine
1/4 cup minced onion
1/4 cup chopped mushrooms
1/4 cup walnuts, coarsely ground
1/4 cup pitted prunes, cut into small pieces
1 tbs. chopped parsley
3/4 tsp. poultry seasoning
1-1/2 cups soft bread crumbs
1/8 tsp. freshly ground white pepper
1 egg, lightly beaten
1/2 cup beef bouillon or red table wine
3/4 cup water

Trim visible fat from meat. Sprinkle with 1/4 teaspoon salt and pepper. Pound

steak or score lightly on both sides. Melt margarine in cooker and add onions. When onions begin to show color, add mushrooms. Continue to sauté just until golden brown. Add nuts, prunes, parsley, poultry seasoning, bread crumbs, 1/4 teaspoon salt, pepper and egg. Stir to blend. Add bouillon and blend again. Remove from heat. Taste and adjust seasoning if necessary. Spread dressing over flank steak. Roll as you would a jelly roll. Tie at 2-inch intervals to secure. If needed, add a little more margarine or vegetable oil to cooker and brown meat. Add water. Cover and set control at 10. Cook 35 minutes after control jiggles. (For cookers having 15 pound setting only, decrease cooking time 10 minutes.) Reduce pressure normally 5 minutes, then place cooker under cold running water. Thicken gravy as desired. Makes 6 servings.

Consider all specified cooking times as guides because the age of fresh vegetables and fruits, grade and shape of meat and amount of bone all tend to give varying results.

SAN FRANCISCO BEEF BURGUNDY

2 lbs. chuck or rump of beef
1/2 lb. fresh mushroom
4 tbs. vegetable oil
1/4 lb. salt pork, sliced thin
1 tsp. salt
1/2 tsp. freshly ground pepper
1/4 cup green onions or scallions
1/2 tsp. oregano
1/2 tsp. minced garlic
1-1/4 cup finely chopped carrots
2 cups Burgundy wine
1/3 cup cognac
1 tbs. tomato paste
parsley sprigs

Cut meat in 1-1/2 inch cubes. Set aside. Wash and slice mushroom and saute´ in oil in uncovered cooker. Remove from cooker and set aside. Brown salt pork in cooker.

Remove and set aside. Pour out all but 3 tablespoons fat from cooker and brown meat. Season with salt and pepper. Add remaining ingredients except tomato paste and parsley. Cover and set control at 10. Cook 25 minutes after control jiggles. (For cookers having 15 pound setting only, decrease cooking time 5 minutes.) Reduce pressure normally 5 minutes, then place cooker under cold running water. Transfer meat to warm serving dish. Add mushrooms to cooker. Stir in tomato paste. Correct seasoning, and pour gravy over beef. Garnish with parsley. (If thickened gravy is desired, follow directions given below. Add mushrooms and tomato paste after gravy thickens.) Makes 6 servings.

Note: When a thickened gravy is desired, measure pan broth and pour into a small saucepan or make in cooker if space allows. For each cup of gravy measure 1/4 cup water into a small jar or container with a lid. Add 2 tablespoons flour. Cover and shake until blended. Strain into simmering broth and cook over medium heat, stirring, until gravy boils. Correct seasoning. Serve in a gravy boat or spooned over meat.

For an additional treat, add minced parsley and four slices of crisp, crumbled bacon to gravy.

BEEF POT ROAST

This popular standby lends itself to multiple uses and variations.

1 (about 3 lbs.) boneless chuck or rump roast
3 tbs. flour
1-1/2 tsp. salt
1/4 tsp. pepper
3 tbs. vegetable oil
1/2 cup chopped onion
1/2 cup water
1/2 cup red table wine

Trim visible fat from roast. Combine flour, salt and pepper in paper bag. Add meat and shake vigorously to coat well. Heat oil in cooker. Brown meat thoroughly on all sides. Add onion, water and wine. Cover and set control at 10. Cook 45 to 60 minutes after control jiggles. (For cookers having 15 pound setting only, decrease cooking time 10 to 15 minutes.) Reduce pressure normally 5 minutes, then place cooker under cold running water. Thicken pan juices (see page 53) if desired. Makes 4 to 6 servings.

Variations

For a West Indies version, omit red table wine and increase water to 1 cup. Add 1 clove garlic, 1/2 teaspoon thyme, 1 cup canned tomatoes, undrained, and 1/2 teaspoon powdered ginger.

For a Continental flavor, omit red wine and increase water to 1 cup. Add 2 tablespoons caraway seed and 1/2 cup vinegar.

For an herbal variety, add 1/2 teaspoon oregano, 1 bay leaf, crumbled, 1/2 clove garlic, 1/4 teaspoon thyme and 8 whole cloves.

Bring pressure up over high or medium heat then reduce immediately when control begins to jiggle.

HEARTY BEEF STEW

1-1/2 lbs. lean stewing beef
2 tbs. margarine
1/2 tsp. salt
1/4 tsp. freshly ground pepper
1/4 tsp. allspice
1 bay leaf
1 cup water
1/2 cup red table wine
1/3 cup onion, chopped fine
4 whole carrots
1 stalk celery with leaves, cut in half
2 white turnips, quartered
2 potatoes, halved
2 tbs. sour cream

Cut meat in 1-1/2 inch pieces. Heat margarine in cooker and brown meat. Sprinkle with salt, pepper and allspice. Add bay leaf, water and wine. Cover and set control at

10. Cook 15 minutes after control jiggles. (For cookers having 15 pound setting only decrease cooking time 3 minutes.) Reduce pressure normally 5 minutes, then complete under cold running water. Remove cover and add onion, carrots, celery, turnips and potatoes. Cover and set control at 15. Cook 8 minutes after control jiggles. Reduce pressure at once by placing cooker under cold running water. Remove meat and vegetables to warmed platter. Cover with foil to keep hot. With large spoon, skim off fat and drain pan juices from cooker. Measure 1-1/2 cups and return to cooker. (Refrigerate remainder for future use.) With wire whisk beat in sour cream one tablespoon at a time. Heat slowly, being careful not to let boil. Correct seasoning and pour over meat and vegetables. Serve at once. Makes 4 servings.

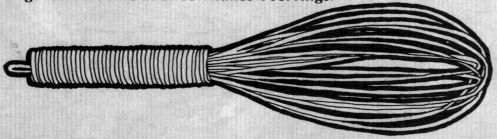

MARINATED BEEF SHORT RIBS

Easy to prepare in the morning for evening use.

Zesty Marinade, page 59
3 lbs. beef short ribs
2 tbs. bacon drippings
2 tbs. onion, sliced paper-thin
2 tbs. green bell pepper, chopped
water
2 tbs. flour
2 tbs. cold water

Prepare marinade. Trim short ribs and place in deep bowl. Pour marinade over them. Cover and let stand 6 hours turning at least twice. Remove ribs and pour marinade into a 2-cup measure. Add water, to make 2 cups liquid. Heat bacon drippings in cooker. Brown ribs until deep golden. Pour off excess fat. Add measured marinade. Cover and set control at 10. Cook 35 to 45 minutes after control jiggles. (For cookers having 15 pound setting only, decrease cooking time 5 minutes.) Reduce

pressure normally 5 minutes, then place cooker under cold running water. Skim off fat. Thicken pan juices with flour and water which have been mixed together, stirring until smooth. Boil 2 minutes and serve with ribs. Makes 6 servings.

Zesty Marinade

1 cup catsup
1 tsp. salt
1/2 tsp. celery seed
2 tbs. brown sugar
2 tbs. lemon juice
1/4 tsp. chili powder
2 tbs. prepared mustard

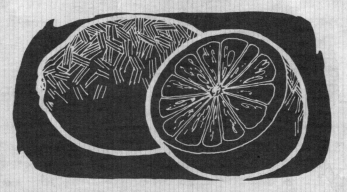

   Mix all indredients together and pour over meat. Cover and refrigerate several hours, turning meat at least twice. Drain and reserve marinade for later use. Makes enough marinade to season 3 pounds meat or 2 pounds chicken.

59

VIENNESE "BOILED" DINNER

2 lbs. beef brisket
1-1/2 tsp. salt
1 bay leaf
4 whole peppercorns
2 whole allspice
1 cup water

1 lb. chicken parts (neck, back, wings)
1 medium onion, sliced
6 carrots halved lengthwise
3 stalks celery, cut into 2-inch pieces
2 large potatoes, quartered
parsley

Trim visible fat from brisket and place in cooker. Add salt, bay leaf, peppercorns, allspice and water. Cover and set control at 10. Cook 40 minutes after control jiggles. (For cookers having 15 pound setting only, decrease cooking time 10 minutes). Reduce pressure normally 5 minutes, then place cooker under cold running water. Uncover and measure pan juices. Add water to make 1-1/2 cups. Pour into cooker and add chicken parts. Cover and set control at 15. Cook 15 to 20 minutes after control jiggles. Reduce pressure normally 5 minutes then place cooker under cold running water. Meanwhile cook vegetables together in saucepan in lightly salted water. Drain well. Place meat and chicken on warm serving platter. Circle with cooked vegetables. Keep warm. Thicken pan juices and spoon over all. Garnish with parsley. Makes 6 to 8 servings.

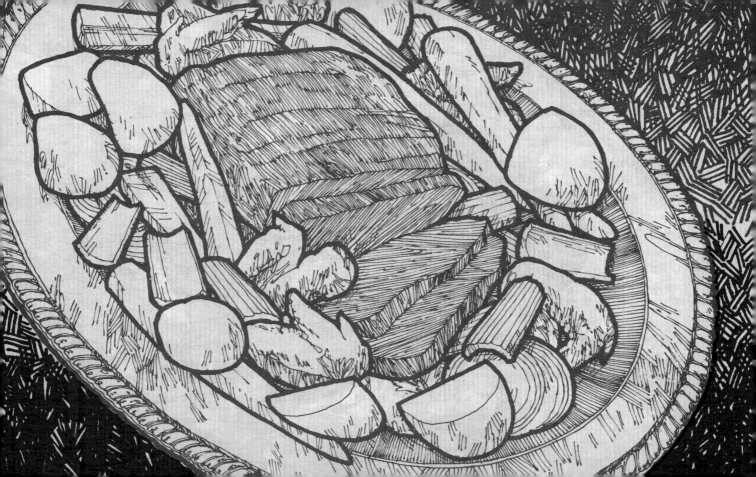

BEEF TONGUE WITH RAISIN SAUCE

Delicious served hot or cold. If serving hot, make the sauce while tongue is cooking. A noodle ring is an excellent choice for a side dish.

1 (about 3 lbs.) fresh beef tongue*
2 cups water
2 tsp. salt
1 bay leaf
1 carrot, sliced
1 onion, studded with 4 cloves
1 stalk celery with leaves
Raisin Sauce, page 63

Wash tongue and drain. Place in cooker. Pour in water and add salt, bay leaf, carrot, onion and celery. Cover and set control at 10. Cook 60 minutes after control jiggles. (For cooker having 15 pound setting only, decrease cooking time 15 minutes.) Cool normally for 5 minutes, then place cooker under cold running water. Uncover and remove tongue. Peel off skin. Slice and serve with Raisin Sauce. Makes 6 to 8 servings.

Raisin Sauce

1/2 cup blanched, slivered almonds
2 cups water
2/3 cup seedless raisins
6 tbs. margarine

3 tbs. flour
1/3 cup crushed gingersnaps
1 tsp. grated lemon rind

Combine almonds and water in a small saucepan. Simmer over low heat 20 minutes. Add raisins and simmer 20 minutes longer. Drain raisins and almonds, reserving the liquid. Melt margarine and blend in flour. Pour in about 2 tablespoons of the hot reserved liquid and stir until smooth. Add additional water to reserved liquid to make 3 cups. Add to flour mixture. Cook, stirring, until thickened. Stir in gingersnaps, lemon rind, raisins and almonds. Correct seasoning. Spoon over tongue slices at time of serving. Makes 3 cups sauce.

*A corned tongue may be used instead of a fresh one, if desired. Omit salt.

HAWAIIAN PINEAPPLE VEAL PATTIES

1 lb. ground veal
2 tbs. bread crumbs
2 tbs. tomato juice
1 tsp. instant onion flakes
1/2 tsp. salt
1/8 tsp. freshly ground pepper
1/8 tsp. thyme

1 egg, slightly beaten
3 tbs. vegetable oil
4 thick slices pineapple
1/2 cup water
1/4 cup brown sugar
1/2 cup pineapple syrup

Combine meat, bread crumbs, tomato juice, seasonings and egg. Shape into 4 rounded patties. Heat 2 tablespoons oil in cooker. Brown patties lightly on both sides. Remove patties from cooker. Quickly brown pineapple and remove. Place rack in cooker and pour in water. Place patties on rack and top each with a slice of browned pineapple. In small mixing bowl combine brown sugar, pineapple syrup and remaining 1 tablespoon oil. Spoon over patties. Cover and set control at 10. Cook 10 minutes after control jiggles. (For cookers having 15 pound setting only, decrease cooking time 3 minutes.) Reduce pressure normally 5 minutes, then complete by placing under cold running water. Makes 4 servings.

VEAL STEAKS WITH MUSHROOMS

Mashed potatoes, a vegetable and molded fruit salad go well with this entree.

veal steak (about 1-1/4 lbs.)
1/2 tsp. salt
1/8 tsp. freshly ground pepper
1/3 cup flour
1 tbs. vegetable oil

1 bouillon cube
1/2 tsp. paprika
3/4 cup water
4 large mushrooms
1/3 cup sour cream

Cut steak into 4 serving size pieces. Season with salt and pepper and dredge in flour. Heat oil in cooker and brown veal well. Add bouillon cube, paprika and water. Cover and set control at 10. Cook 18 to 20 minutes after control jiggles. (For cookers having 15 pound setting only, decrease cooking time 3 to 5 minutes.) Reduce pressure normally 5 minutes, then place cooker under cold running water. Slice mushrooms paper thin and add to cooker. Heat thoroughly without covering. Measure out about 1/2 cup liquid and blend with sour cream. Return to cooker and heat but do not boil. Serve steaks on warm plates and spoon sauce over each portion. Makes 4 servings.

VEAL AND HAM ROLLS

4 veal cutlets or steaks
1 can (4-1/2 ozs.) deviled ham
1/2 cup stuffed green olives, sliced
1 tbs. instant minced onion
1 pkg. (3 ozs.) cream cheese
1 egg, slightly beaten

1/2 cup dry bread crumbs
2 tbs. margarine
1/2 cup water
1 can (2-1/2 ozs.) Franco American
   Mushroom Gravy
1 tbs. each sweet and dry vermouth, blended

Pound meat very thin. Mix deviled ham, olives, minced onion and cream cheese. Spread evenly over cutlets. Roll veal like jelly rolls and fasten with toothpicks. Dip rolls in egg. Then in bread crumbs. Heat margarine in cooker. Add rolls and brown on all sides. Turn fold-side down and pour water into cooker. Cover and set control at 10. Cook 10 to 15 minutes after control jiggles. (For cookers having 15 pound setting only, decrease cooking time 1 to 2 minutes.) Reduce pressure normally 5 minutes, then place cooker under cold running water. Combine gravy and vermouth. Heat and spoon over rolls. Serve with rice or stuffed baked potatoes. Makes 4 servings.

TWO-STEP PORK CHOPS

4 (about 1/2 in. thick) pork chops
1 tbs. vegetable oil
4 thick slices Bermuda onion
1 cup uncooked long grain rice
4 thick slices tomato

4 thick slices green pepper
1-1/2 cups tomato juice
1/4 cup red table wine
parsley

Trim all visible fat from chops. Heat oil in cooker and brown chops well on both sides. Remove chops and add onion slices. Cook 2 minutes. Remove onions and add rice. Stir constantly until brown. Remove rice and place rack in cooker. Arrange chops on rack. Top each chop with a mound of rice and a slice each of tomato, green pepper and onion. Press gently into rice. Carefully pour in tomato juice and wine. Cover and set control at 10. Cook 12 minutes after control jiggles. (For cookers having 15 pound setting only, decrease cooking time 3 minutes.) Reduce pressure normally 5 minutes then place cooker under cold running water. Remove cover and lift pork chops and toppings out carefully. Garnish with parsley. Makes 4 servings.

ESTONIAN SAUERKRAUT WITH PORK

The week before New Year's is as festive in Estonia as it is throughout the U.S.S.R. It is the time of "Christmas trees," Grandfather Frost and jollity. And because the winters are especially severe in this little country that faces on the Gulf of Finland, hearty fare is the rule.

An Estonian friend, Linda Timre, who shared this recipe with me when I was in Tallinn, tells me that this is a "must" specialty of the season. She emphasizes that the sauerkraut must be made one week ahead to ripen. Serve this traditional dish with hash brown or fried potatoes to be authentic.

1 cabbage
2 tbs. sugar
1 tbs. salt
1/2 tsp. caraway seed
1 lb. salt pork

To make sauerkraut, wash cabbage, trim and remove core. Shred coarsely into large mixing bowl. Add sugar, salt and caraway. Mash with a potato masher or use a

food mill to extract as much juice as possible from cabbage mixture. Cover and let stand at least one week to ferment. When ready to prepare the final dish, cut salt pork into 1-1/2 inch pieces. Sauté in cooker until golden. Remove and add rack to cooker. Place salt pork on rack and top with slightly drained sauerkraut. Add 3/4 cup sauerkraut juice. Cover and set control at 15. Cook 4 minutes after control jiggles. Reduce pressure normally 5 minutes then place cooker under cold running water. Makes 4 servings.

Variation

Slice cabbage for sauerkraut in thin slices instead of shredding. When adding to browned salt pork, also add 2 peeled potatoes, cut in fourths or eighths, depending on size. Cover and set control at 15. Cook 6 minutes after control jiggles. Reduce pressure normally 5 minutes, then place cooker under cold running water.

SOUTH OF THE BORDER PORK

2 tbs. vegetable oil
2 lbs. pork shoulder (or loin) sliced thin
1 clove garlic, mashed
1 tbs. lemon juice
1/3 cup orange juice
1/2 tsp. sugar
1-1/2 tsp. Worcestershire sauce
1 tsp. salt
1/8 tsp. pepper
1 cup water

Heat oil in cooker over moderate heat. Brown pork slices and garlic. Remove garlic and discard. Add remaining ingredients. Cover and set control at 10. Cook 15 minutes after control jiggles. (For cookers having 15 pound setting only, decrease cooking time 3 minutes.) Reduce pressure normally 5 minutes. Then place cooker under cold running water. Uncover pan juices and correct seasoning. Serve with rice or mashed potatoes. Spoon pan juices over top. Makes 6 generous servings.

ESTONIAN ONE-POT "FOOD"

This old time recipe is hearty enough for a main dish just as the name suggests. Serve in soup bowls with dark bread, marinated cucumbers or tossed salad and a simple dessert, and you have a balanced meal with little effort. Adapted for American kitchens, this is how you make Meta Terri's One Pot "Food" in a pressure cooker.

2 tbs. vegetable oil
3 lbs. lamb (or mutton) shanks
1 qt. water
1 tsp. salt

12 cabbage leaves, quartered
6 small carrots, cut in half
6 potatoes, cut into small pieces
1/2 tsp. or more caraway seed

Heat oil in cooker and brown shanks. Sprinkle with 1/2 teaspoon salt. Add water and cover. Set control at 15. Cook 45 minutes after control jiggles. Reduce pressure normally 5 minutes, then place cooker under cold running water. Remove meat from cooker and shred. Return meat to cooker along with vegetables, remaining salt and caraway. Cover and set control at 15. Cook 6 minutes after control jiggles. Reduce pressure normally 5 minutes, then complete under cold running water. Correct seasonings. Serve at once. Makes 6 to 8 servings.

Chicken For Everyday And Sunday

Chicken is so delicious and versatile it is bound to please whether used as fancy fare for parties or simply prepared for family meals. It is good for lunches too as sandwich fillers or in julianne strips or cubes for salads. Moreover it is available all year round and is less expensive and lower in fat content than meat.

If you buy fresh chicken to freeze for later use, do not keep longer than a few months for maximum flavor and quality. Fresh poultry should not be kept longer than two days before cooking.

Don't be afraid to experiment with your own recipes. To adapt them to the pressure cooker, follow a few simple procedures:

1. Apply cooking time, amount of liquid and method of reducing pressure, taken from charts or recipes in this section or manufacturer's handbook, to your recipes.

2. If your recipe calls for wine, juice or soup stock, consider this as part of liquid requirement specified in a basic or similar pressure cooker recipe.

3. When you want a crispy outer finish to chicken, brown before cooking.

4. If additional brownness or crispness is desired, place chicken under broiler 2 or 3 minutes after taking from cooker.

CHICKEN WITH APRICOT GLAZE

1 (about 3 lbs.) frying chicken
2 tbs. sherry
1/4 tsp. salt
1/8 tsp. savory
2 tbs. vegetable oil
1 cup water

1 small onion
    or 1 tsp. instant minced onion
1/3 cup apricot preserves
1/4 tsp. prepared mustard
1/4 tsp. allspice
1/3 cup orange juice

Cut chicken into serving pieces. Wipe pieces with damp cloth and pat dry with paper towel. Brush cavity with sherry and rub with salt and savory. Heat oil in cooker. Brown chicken until golden on all sides. Slip rack under chicken. Add water and onion. Cover and set control at 10. Cook 18 to 25 minutes after control jiggles. (For cookers having 15 pound setting only, decrease cooking time 3 to 5 minutes.) Reduce pressure normally 5 minutes, then complete under cold running water. Uncover and transfer chicken to broiler pan. Paint all surfaces of chicken with a glaze made by mixing apricot preserves, mustard, allspice and orange juice together. Broil 2 to 3 minutes to crisp and brown. Watch carefully as glaze is apt to scorch. Remove and serve at once. Makes 4 servings.

CHICKEN TARRAGON

The seasoning makes the difference.

1 (3 to 3-1/2 lbs.) frying chicken
2 to 3 tbs. flour
1/2 to 1 tsp. dried tarragon,
    crumbled between fingers
1/8 tsp. white pepper

1 tsp. paprika
3 tbs. vegetable oil
1 small onion
1 cup water

Wipe chicken with damp cloth. Pat dry with paper towel. Cut into serving pieces and remove skin. In paper bag mix flour, tarragon, salt, pepper and paprika. Add chicken and shake until well coated. Brown in hot oil in cooker. Slip rack under chicken. Add onion and water. Cover and set control at 10. Cook 15 to 20 minutes after control jiggles. (For cookers having 15 pound setting only, decrease cooking time 2 minutes.) Reduce pressure normally 5 minutes then place cooker under cold running water. Transfer chicken to broiler pan and broil 2 to 3 minutes to crisp. Serve with giblet gravy (page 89) or heated undiluted mushroom soup. Makes 4 servings.

MANDARIN BARBECUED CHICKEN

1 (about 3 lbs.) frying chicken
1/2 tsp. grated orange peel
1/2 tsp. grated lemon peel
1/4 cup orange juice
1/4 cup lemon juice
1/3 cup vegetable oil
2 tbs. Worcestershire sauce

1/4 tsp. oregano leaves, crushed
1/4 tsp. rosemary, crushed
1/4 tsp. freshly ground pepper
1 clove garlic, crushed (optional)
1 tsp. salt
1 tbs. margarine

Wipe chicken with damp cloth and pat dry with paper towel. Cut into serving pieces and remove skin. Place chicken in bowl. Combine remaining ingredients except margarine and pour over chicken. Cover and refrigerate 5 to 6 hours. Turn pieces occasionally. Heat margarine in cooker and brown chicken. Slip rack under chicken. Add water to marinade to make 1 cup. Pour over chicken. Cover and set control at 10. Cook 18 to 25 minutes after control jiggles. (For cookers having 15 pound setting only, decrease cooking time 3 to 5 minutes.) Transfer chicken to broiler pan. Brush with pan juices and broil 2 to 3 minutes to crisp. Makes 4 servings.

CHICKEN CHOW MEIN

2 whole chicken breasts*
2 tbs. vegetable oil
1 cup water
1/2 cup onions, sliced
2-1/2 cups celery, cut
   in 2 in. diagonal slices

1/2 tsp. salt
1/8 tsp. white pepper
2 tbs. cornstarch
1/2 cup water
1/4 cup soy sauce

2 cups fresh bean sprouts
   or 1 can (1 lb. 4 ozs.)
1/2 cup mushrooms
1 can (8 ozs.) water chestnuts
   sliced paper-thin

Bone and skin chicken. Cut into strips and brown in oil in cooker until golden. Add water, onions, celery, salt and pepper. Cover and set control at 10. Cook 10 minutes after control jiggles. (For cookers having 15 pound setting only, decrease cooking time 2 minutes.) Reduce pressure normally for 5 minutes, then place cooker under cold running water. Blend cornstarch and water in a saucepan. Add soy sauce, bean sprouts, mushrooms and water chestnuts. Cook over medium heat until mixture thickens, stirring constantly so that sauce is smooth. Make a bed of hot rice on each plate. Spoon chicken over rice and top with bean sprout sauce. Makes 4 servings.

*Pork cubes or strips may be used instead of chicken. Be sure to brown well.

RED-COOKED GINGER CHICKEN

A treat for the eye as well as for taste.

1 (about 3 lbs.) frying chicken
2 slices fresh ginger root
1 scallion and stalk
2 cloves anise
2 in. piece cinnamon stick
2 white peppercorns
3 tbs. vegetable oil (preferably sesame)
1 cup water
1/4 cup soy sauce
1/4 cup dry sherry
1 tsp. brown sugar

Wipe chicken pieces with damp cloth and pat dry with paper towel. Skin if desired. Cut ginger slices into small pieces. Slice scallion stalk into 1 inch slices and the bulb into thin slices. Set aside. Put anise cloves, cinnamon stick and peppercorns into a

78

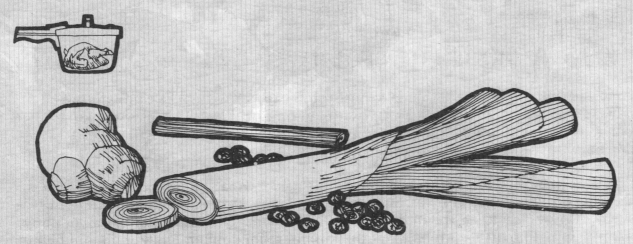

small square of cheesecloth. Bring corners to center and knot securely. Heat oil in cooker and lightly brown chicken. Slip rack under chicken. Pour in water and scatter ginger and scallion over chicken. Place seasoning bag in center. Blend soy sauce, sherry and brown sugar. Add to cooker. Cover and set control at 10. Cook 15 to 20 minutes after control jiggles. (The cooking time is the same for cookers having 15 pound setting only.) Reduce pressure normally 5 minutes, then place cooker under cold running water. Remove seasoning bag and thicken pan juices if gravy is desired. Serve chicken with brown rice. Makes 4 servings.

CORNISH HEN FOR TWO

1 tbs. melted margarine
2 tbs. frozen juice
    concentrate, undiluted
2 tbs. vegetable oil

8 mushroom caps
2 tbs. dry vermouth
3/4 tsp. salt

1 Cornish Hen
1 cup water
paprika

Combine margarine and orange juice. Set aside. Heat oil in cooker and brown mushrooms until golden. Remove from cooker and sprinkle with vermouth and 1/4 teaspoon salt. Cover and keep warm. Wipe hen with damp cloth and pat dry with paper towel. Split in half. Brush each half lightly with oil from cooker. Reheat oil and brown meaty side of halves until golden. Turn and cook 5 minutes. Turn breast side up and slip rack underneath. Brush each half with orange glaze and sprinkle with remaining salt. Pour water into cooker. Cover and set control at 10. Cook 15 to 20 minutes after control jiggles. (For cookers having 15 pound setting only, decrease cooking time 3 to 5 minutes.) Reduce pressure normally 5 minutes, then place cooker under cold running water. Place hen halves on broiler pan. Brush with remaining glaze and sprinkle with paprika. Broil about 5 minutes until brown and crisp. Arrange mushrooms on 2 warm plates and top with Cornish hen halves. Garnish as desired. Makes 2 servings.

"ROASTED" CHICKEN WITH DRESSING

Apricot Dressing, page 83
1 (4 lbs.) roasting chicken
1/4 cup flour
1/8 tsp. white pepper
1/8 tsp. savory

1 tsp. paprika
1 tsp. salt
1/4 cup vegetable oil
1 cup water
1/4 cup white table wine

Prepare dressing. Wipe chicken with a damp cloth and pat dry with paper towel. Combine flour, pepper, savory and paprika in a paper bag. Add chicken. Close and shake vigorously to dredge well. Heat oil in cooker and brown chicken evenly on all sides. Remove and lightly salt outside, but not cavity. Stuff chicken just before cooking. Avoid overpacking. Cavity should never be more than 3/4 full to allow for expansion. Close opening with small skewers and criss crossed string. Fasten legs close to body by tying drumsticks together. Fill neck cavity loosely with remaining dressing. Bring skin over opening and tie with string around neck leaving long ends. Turn wings under back and pass string ends around them and tie. Add rack, water and wine to cooker. Place chicken breast-side up on rack. Cover and set control at 10. Cook 25 to 30 minutes after control jiggles. (For cookers having 15 pound setting only, decrease

cooking time 5 minutes.) **Reduce pressure normally 5 minutes then place cooker under cold running water to complete. Uncover and transfer chicken to broiler pan. Broil 2 to 3 minutes to crisp and brown. Remove stuffing and carve chicken. Serve with giblet gravy (page 89). Makes 4 servings.**

Apricot Dressing

4 dried apricots
boiling water
1 cup (1/2 6-oz. pkg.) Stove Top
    Cornbread Stuffing Crumbs

1/2 packet vegetable seasoning
2 tbs. margarine, softened
3/4 cup hot water

    Soak apricots in water 1/2 hour. Drain and cut into very small pieces. Toss with crumbs. Mix seasoning, margarine and water in mixing bowl. Add crumbs and stir lightly just to moisten. For drier stuffing use a few more crumbs.
    Note: For hearty eaters prepare the whole package of dressing. Bake the half not used for stuffing in 1-1/2 quart casserole, uncovered, in 400°F oven 15 minutes.

CHICKEN FRICASSEE WITH HERB DUMPLINGS

1 (about 3 lbs.) stewing chicken
salt
white pepper
2 tbs. vegetable oil
1-1/2 cups water
1 tbs. instant minced onion
Herb Dumplings, page 85

Wipe chicken with damp cloth. Pat dry with paper towel. Cut into serving pieces. Season with salt and pepper. Heat oil in cooker. Brown chicken. Add water and onion. Cover and set control at 10. Cook 20 to 25 minutes after control jiggles. (For cookers having 15 pound setting only, decrease cooking time 10 to 15 minutes.) Reduce pressure normally 5 minutes, then place cooker under cold running water. Remove cover and drop dumpling batter by teaspoonfuls on top of simmering chicken. Cook uncovered 5 minutes. Cover and steam 5 minutes without control on vent. Remove dumplings and chicken to warm platter. Measure broth. Make gravy using 2 tablespoons flour and 1/4 cup water, blended together, for each cup of broth. Cook until

gravy boils and thickens. Serve over chicken and dumplings. Makes 4 servings.

Herb Dumplings

1-1/2 cups all-purpose flour
2 tsp. baking powder
1/2 tsp. salt
pinch sugar
1/4 tsp. thyme
1/4 tsp. powdered savory
1 egg
1/2 cup milk

Sift dry ingredients together. Beat egg and milk. Combine mixtures, stirring thoroughly to blend. Drop dumpling batter by teaspoonfuls onto simmering chicken. Cook uncovered 5 minutes. Cover and steam 5 minutes without control on vent. Makes 4 servings. Herb Dumplings are also delicious with beef stew.

WHOLE CHICKEN FRICASSEE

1 (about 3 lbs.) whole stewing chicken
4 tbs. flour
1 tsp. salt
1/4 tsp. white pepper
2 tbs. vegetable oil
1 carrot

1 bay leaf
1 stalk celery
1 chicken bouillon cube
1 cup water
1/2 cup white table wine

Wash chicken and giblets. Pat dry with paper towel. Put 2 tablespoons flour, salt and pepper into paper bag. Add chicken and giblets. Shake vigorously to coat well. Heat oil in cooker. Brown chicken and giblets until golden. Add remaining ingredients except flour. Cover cooker and set control at 10. Cook 30 to 40 minutes after control jiggles. (For cookers having 15 pound setting only, decrease cooking time 10 minutes.) Reduce pressure normally 5 minutes then complete under cold running water. Remove chicken to warm platter. Chop giblets. Blend remaining flour with 3 to 4 tablespoons water. Add to cooker and stir until smoothly blended. Cook, stirring, until gravy boils and thickens. Add giblets. Ladle over chicken and serve with mashed potatoes or rice. Makes 4 servings.

CHICKEN NOODLE CUSTARD

Bright green peas with sliced water chestnuts added complement this dish.

1 cup milk
2 eggs
1/2 tsp. savory powder
1/8 tsp. curry powder
1/2 tsp. salt
1/8 tsp. white pepper
1/2 cup hot chicken bouillon

2/3 cup cooked wide noodles
1-1/3 cups cooked chicken, page 88
1/4 cup ricotta cheese
2 tbs. white table wine, optional
paprika
1 cup water

Heat milk but do not boil. Lightly beat eggs in large bowl. Stir in seasonings, hot milk and bouillon. Add cooked noodles, chicken, cheese and wine. Turn mixture into a lightly oiled 1 quart casserole. Sprinkle with paprika. Cover casserole with a double fold of foil. Crimp edges to secure or tie with string. Place rack in cooker and add water. Set casserole on rack. Cover and set control at 5. Cook 5 minutes after control jiggles. (For cookers having 15 pound setting only, decrease cooking time 3 minutes.) Reduce pressure normally. Serve immediately. Makes 6 servings.

STEAMED CHICKEN

Deliciously tender for making chicken curry, casseroles, salad, pies, a la king and many other dishes calling for cooked chicken. For an extra treat make gravy with the giblets to use now or freeze.

1 (3 to 4 lbs.) stewing chicken
1 unpeeled carrot, scrubbed
1 large celery stalk with leaves
1 small onion
1 tsp. salt

3 white peppercorns
1/2 tsp. savory
pinch dried tarragon
1-1/2 cups water

Cut chicken in quarters. Wipe with damp cloth and place in cooker with remaining ingredients. Cover and set control at 10. Cook 15 to 20 minutes after control jiggles. (For cookers having 15 pound setting only, decrease cooking time 2 minutes.) Reduce pressure normally 5 minutes then place cooker under cold running water. Lift chicken pieces from cooker and refrigerate. Strain broth and refrigerate. (Use within 2 or 3 days or freeze.) When chicken is cool enough to handle remove meat from bones in as large pieces as possible. Discard skin and bones. Cover chicken and refrigerate. Use within 2

days or freeze. Makes about 2-1/2 cups cubed chicken.

Giblet Gravy

chicken giblets and neck	1/4 cup flour
salted water to cover	salt
1/4 tsp. instant minced onion	freshly ground pepper
1/4 cup margarine or pan drippings	2 tbs. dry sherry

Place washed giblets and neck in saucepan with salted water and onion. Cover and simmer until tender. Drain and measure broth. Add water if necessary to make 2 cups liquid. Cool giblets and chop. Discard neck. Melt margarine in pan or heat drippings left in cooker if making giblet gravy for chicken that was browned before cooking. Add flour and cook, stirring, 1 to 2 minutes. Stir in giblet broth. Cook over medium heat, stirring constantly, until gravy thickens. Add chopped giblets, salt, pepper and sherry. Reheat. If a richer gravy is desired add 1/2 cup half and half. Makes about 3 cups.

Fish, A Many Splendored Food

Fish is a bounty food. High in protein and other nutrients, it is low in waste so is generally cheaper than meat, pound for pound. Exeptions are abalone, salmon and shellfish.

Except for the mercury scare a few years ago, fish has been given a clean bill of health. It appears on many diet lists for use six or more times a week in place of meat (which is higher in saturated fat) and as a trade-off with poultry choices.

Buy fresh fish whenever possible and buy it only when it smells fresh. Avoid any fish that is stong or fishy in odor. Pop your fish purchase into refrigerator until time of use, and try to make this the day of purchase. If frozen fish is partially defrosted, do not refreeze, but use at once.

In the average market you will find such cuts of fish as:

Fillets — side of fish, cut lenthwise away from bone. Ready to cook.

Steaks — cross sections from a large dressed fish, cut about 1/2 to 1 inch thick.

Chunks — cross sections of large dressed fish; a cross section of the backbone is the only bone in a chunk.

Because fish has less fat than meat, you'll find that it cooks quickly in your cooker and will give excellent results.

Fish is classified as fat or lean. Among the most popular so-called fat fish are:

bluefish halibut mackerel

Lean fish are:

carp haddock trout sole flounder

Fish may be prepared in cooker by two methods:

1. Wrap fish in cheese cloth before cooking to guard against it falling apart.
2. If browned crustiness is desired, roll fish in flour, cornmeal or fish fry. Brown in cooker before covering to steam-cook.

Plan colorful, chewey vegetables for color and taste contrast when fish is to be your main dish. Try red cabbage wedges, celery and tomatoes, cucumber slices, radishes or carrots. Peas and green beans too if you combine them with slices of water chestnuts or slivered nutmeats. Be imaginative with seasonings when preparing fish. Try basil, bay, capers, crushed fennel, onion, thyme, dill, ginger, garlic, white pepper and a parade of others. And use a white table wine to enhance the whole.

HALIBUT STEAKS CONTINENTAL

3/4 cup seedless white grapes
1/4 cup dry vermouth
1-1/2 lbs. halibut, perch, turbot
   or other thickly sliced white fish
2 tbs. margarine
cheesecloth

1 tsp. salt
1/8 tsp. white pepper
1 tbs. instant minced onion
1/2 cup water
1 cup medium cream sauce, page 147

Peel 1/2 cup grapes and pour vermouth over them. Cut fish into serving pieces. Brown in cooker in melted margarine. Carfully remove fish from cooker and lay on piece of cheesecloth large enough to cover. Season with salt and pepper. Sprinkle with onions, peeled grapes and vermouth. Bring corners of cheesecloth together and tie so it holds fish securely. Return to cooker and add water. Cover and set control at 10. Cook 5 minutes after control jiggles. (For cookers having 15 pound setting only, drecrease cooking time 1 minutes.) Reduce pressure at once by placing under cold running water. Unwrap fish and place on warm platter. Spoon cream sauce over top and garnish with remaining grapes. Makes 4 to 5 servings.

FISH STROGANOFF

Serve with a salad or crisp spinach leaves and sliced raw mushrooms, dressed with oil and fresh lemon juice.

1 lb. halibut or other white fish, sliced 1/2-inch thick
1/2 tsp. salt
1/8 tsp. white pepper
1/4 tsp. dill weed
1/2 onion, sliced

1/4 cup white table wine
3/4 cup water
1/2 tsp. ginger
1 cup sour cream

Season fish slices with salt, pepper and dill weed. Place on rack in cooker with onion, wine and water. Cover and set control at 10. Cook 5 to 6 minutes after control jiggles. (For cookers having 15 pound setting only, decrease cooking time 1 minute.) Reduce pressure at once by putting cooker under cold running water. Remove to warm platter and sprinkle with ginger. Pass sour cream. Makes 4 servings.

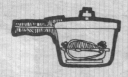

HURRY-UP SHRIMP AND RICE

1 pkg. (5 ozs.) M.J.B. Brown and Wild Rice
1-1/2 cups water
2 tbs. margarine
2 tbs. lemon juice
1/2 lb. cooked deveined shrimp

3/4 cup sliced mushrooms
1 can (10-3/4 ozs.) tomato soup
1/2 cup cream
1/4 cup sherry
1/2 cup chopped cashews

Pour rice into a lightly oiled, 1-quart aluminum mold. Add water, 1 tablespoon margarine and rice seasonings. Place rack in cooker and pour in 2 cups water. Set mold on rack. Cover and set control at 5. Cook 35 minutes after control jiggles. (For cookers having 15 pound setting only, decrease cooking time 10 minutes.) Reduce pressure at once by placing cooker under cold running water. While rice is cooking, pour lemon juice over shrimp in large mixing bowl. Sauté mushrooms in remaining margarine. Add mushrooms, cooked rice, cream and sherry to shrimp. Toss to blend. Stir in soup. Remove rack and water from cooker. Turn rice mixture into cooker. Cover and set control at 5. Cook 1 minutes after control jiggles. (For 15 pound setting, remove from heat as soon as control jiggles.) Reduce pressure normally. Serve topped with nuts. Makes 4 to 6 servings.

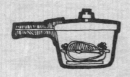

CHINESE FISH AND VEGETABLES

1 pkg. (8 ozs.) fresh Chinese vegetables
1 lb. (1/2-inch thick) white fish fillets
2 tbs. cornstarch
1/2 tsp. salt
1/8 tsp. (scant) cayenne
3 tbs. vegetable oil
1/4 cup fresh ginger root, diced
1 tbs. onion, minced
1 tomato, cut into wedges

3 tbs. chicken broth
1 tbs. soy sauce
1 tbs. dry sherry
1 tsp. sugar
1 tsp. cider vinegar
1 cup water
1 pkg. (10 ozs.) frozen peas, cooked
2 cups hot cooked rice
soy sauce

Thaw Chinese vegetables. Cut fish into 1-inch strips. Coat fish with mixture of 1 tablespoon corstarch, salt and cayenne. Let stand while assembling other ingredients. Heat oil in cooker. Add fish strips and lightly brown. Remove from cooker. Add ginger root, onion and Chinese vegetables. Stir to lightly glaze. Slip rack under vegetables. Lay fish strips on vegetables. Add tomato, broth, soy sauce, sherry, sugar, vinegar and water. Cover and set control at 10. Cook 3 minutes after control jiggles. (For cookers having 15 pound setting only, decrease cooking time 1/2 minute.) Reduce pressure at

once by placing cooker under cold running water. Remove fish and vegetables to warm platter and keep warm. Combine 1 tablespoon cornstarch and 2 tablespoons water. Then add 3 tablespoons pan juices. Stir mixture into cooker. Correct seasoning. Add peas. Heat sauce and pour over hot rice. Serve with fish and vegetables. Pass soy sauce. Makes 4 to 6 servings.

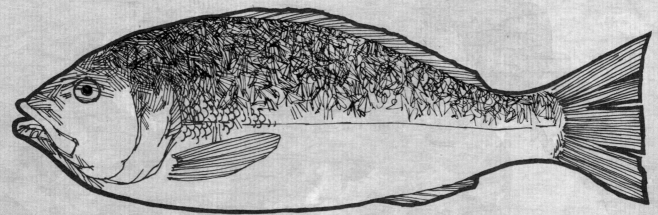

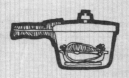

MOUSSAKA WITH TUNA

1 medium eggplant
1/2 cup water
1/3 cup chopped onion
1/4 cup white table wine
2 tbs. cornstrarch
2 cups nonfat milk
1/2 tsp. salt
1/8 tsp. white pepper
1/8 tsp. cinnamon
1/8 tsp. grated nutmeg
1 can (6-1/2 ozs.) tuna
2 eggs, slightly beaten
1 container (8 ozs.) ricotta or cottage cheese
1/2 cup grated Parmesan cheese
1 cup water

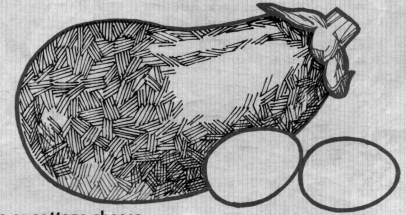

Wash and peel eggplant. Slice about 3/8-inch thick. Drop slices into cooker and add 1/2 cup water. Cover and set control at 15. Cook 1-1/2 minutes after control jiggles. Reduce pressure at once by placing cooker under cold running water. Uncover and place eggplant on paper towels to drain. Put onion and wine in a medium saucepan. Cover and cook over low heat about 5 minutes, until onion is tender. Mix cornstarch with 1/2 cup milk, stirring to smooth. Pour into saucepan. Add remaining milk slowly so that mixture remains velvety. Add seasonings. Continue stirring until mixture bubbles. Remove from heat. Drain tuna and mix with 1/2 cup sauce. Set aside. In medium bowl, beat eggs, ricotta and remaining sauce. Mix thoroughly. Arrange slices of eggplant in aluminum mold or container which will fit into cooker. Cover with some of tuna mixture and sprinkle with Parmesan. Repeat until all have been used. Cover container with two folds of foil and secure by pressing tightly around edges or with string. Place on rack in cooker. Pour in water. Set control at 5 and cook 5 minutes after control jiggles. (For cookers having 15 pound setting only, remove cooker from heat as soon as control jiggles.) If glass or ceramic container is used, increase cooking time to 5-1/2 minutes. Reduce pressure normally. Makes 4 servings.

The Vegetarian Way

Four distinct groups of vegetarians exist in the United States today. One is the Trappist monks who follow a simple way of life. Milk is one of the basics of their diet along with whole grains.

Another group is the Seventh-Day Adventist Church which has devoted much constructive work and research to achieving balanced diets without use of meat, fish or poultry (but eggs and milk are allowed).

The counterculture youth group is also dedicated to a vegetarian diet. Its practices are varied. In some instances members limit the diet to organically grown foods, while others go to the extreme of advocating the Zen macrobiotic diet—a dangerously limiting diet that can lead to serious illness, even death.

A fourth group is a fringe one, composed of people of all ages and beliefs. Some belong to nonviolent groups and practice kindness to animals while others have been long-time vegetarians. Some are older citizens who do not like the "heaviness of meat" while others intersperse meatless meals with those featuring eggs, fish or poultry.

On the pages following we present a galaxy of substantial vegetarian specialties, with the cooker conserving nutrients for you, whatever your beliefs.

ARMENIAN STUFFED CABBAGE LEAVES

1 large cabbage
boiling water
cheesecloth
2 tbs. olive oil
1/4 cup chopped onion
1/2 cup raw rice
1/4 cup finely chopped parsley
2 tbs. raisins
2 tbs. pistachio nuts
2 tbs. tomato paste

1./4 tsp. allspice
1/8 tsp. cinnamon
1 scant tsp. salt
1/4 tsp. freshly ground pepper
1 egg, slightly beaten
3/4 cup chicken stock or
    canned chicken broth
1-1/4 cups water
parsley sprigs
lemon wedges

Pull off tough outer leaves and discard. Cut out bottom core of cabbage with paring knife. Pour boiling water over cabbage and let stand in cooker, uncovered, 5 minutes, or until leaves separate easily. You may use salted or unsalted water for this, according to preference. Remove 1 large leaf and 8 smaller ones. Drain on paper towels and pat dry. Pour oil into cooker and saute′ onion over medium heat until light golden. Pour in rice and stir constantly to keep from scorching. When rice is light

golden brown add remaining ingredients except stock, water, parsley and lemon wedges. Heat through lightly. Place a large square of cheesecloth on a flat surface. In center place a large cabbage leaf, curly edge up. Fit a smaller leaf inside large one and fill smaller one with 1 heaping tablespoon stuffing. Top with another cabbage leaf and stuffing. Repeat until you have used all 8 leaves and stuffing. Bring four corners of cheesecloth together and twist ends to secure. This shapes stuffed leaves into a compact round. Place on rack in cooker and pour in stock and water. Cover and set control at 5. Cook 15 minutes after control jiggles. (For cookers having 15 pound setting only, decrease cooking time 10 minutes.) Reduce pressure instantly by placing cooker under cold running water. Unwrap cabbage and cut into wedges. Garnish with parsley and lemon. Makes 8 servings.

Note: One-half cup finely chopped, cooked chicken makes a nice addition if your diet permits.

ARTICHOKES STUFFED WITH MUSHROOMS

A low calorie combination that is superb in flavor. And you may serve this combination hot or cold.

4 artichokes, pressure cooked, page 124
1-1/4 cups water
1 tsp. salt
1 bay leaf

1-1/2 tbs. cider vinegar
1/2 lb. mushrooms, sliced thin
1/2 tsp. oregano, crumbled fine
1 cup Low Calorie Italian dressing

Prepare artichokes as directed. Refrigerate if serving cold. Bring water, salt, bay leaf and vinegar to rolling boil in cooker. Add mushrooms. Cover and set control at 15. Cook 2 minutes after control jiggles. Reduce pressure at once by placing cooker under cold running water. Drain mushrooms and place in medium mixing bowl. Mix oregano with dressing and pour 1/4 cup over mushrooms. Reserve remaining dressing to pass as a sauce. Serve warm or let stand in refrigerator overnight. Remove center cluster of artichoke leaves and the choke. Fill with mushroom mixture. Makes 4 servings.

BOSTON "BAKED" BEANS

2 cups dried navy beans
water
slices salt pork (about 1/2 lb.)
1-1/2 tbs. minced onions
1/4 cup dark molasses

1/4 cup brown sugar
1 tsp. dry mustard
1 tsp. salt
1/8 tsp. white pepper
2 cups water

Cover beans with water and soak overnight. Drain. Brown salt pork in cooker until light golden. Stir in onions. Add beans and all remaining ingredients. Cover and set control at 15. Cook 25 minutes after control jiggles. Reduce pressure normally. Serve with potato or green salad, Boston brown bread and a milk-containing dessert such as pudding or custard. Makes 4 to 8 servings.

Note: Omit salt pork, if desired, and substitute 1 tablespoon vegetable oil.

Whenever directions call for reducing pressure normally, remove cooker from heat to a cooler part of the range. This is especially important for electric ranges because their units hold heat longer.

GRAPE-NUT AND COTTAGE CHEESE CUSTARD

1 cup grape-nuts
1 cup milk
1/4 cup cottage cheese
2 eggs, slightly beaten
1/2 cup peanuts, ground

1 tsp. instant minced onion
1 tbs. softened margarine
1/2 tsp. celery salt
1 tbs. toasted sesame seed
1-1/2 cups water

Combine all ingredients and stir thoroughly to blend. Correct seasoning. Pour into 4 individual oiled aluminum custard cups or 1-quart aluminum mold. Place rack in cooker and add water. Set molds on rack. Cover and set control at 5. Cook 1 minute after control jiggles. (For cookers having 15 pound setting only, remove cooker from heat when control begins to jiggle.) Reduce pressure normally. Makes 4 servings.

Note: If glass or ceramic custard cups are used instead of aluminum, cook 2-1/2 minutes. If you cover molds be sure to increase cooking time a little.

LIMA BEANS WITH IMITATION BACON

Serve with tossed green or raw vegetable salad and toasted French bread.

2 cups dried lima beans
1 tbs. instant minced onion
1 tsp. salt
3/4 cup diced celery
1 tbs. pimiento strips, chopped

1 can (10-1/4 ozs.) stewed tomatoes
1/4 tsp. sweet basil
1/2 cup water
2 tbs. vegetable oil
1/4 cup imitation bacon bits

Wash beans. Put into large bowl and cover with water. Let stand overnight. Drain. Place beans in cooker with other ingredients except imitation bacon bits. Cover and set control at 15. Cook 25 minutes after control jiggles. Reduce pressure at once by placing cooker under cold running water. Uncover and stir in imitation bacon bits. Serve at once. Makes 4 servings.

Always add oil to frothing foods.

JEWISH NOODLE PUDDING

An old time favorite in our home and one I am sure you will enjoy for its good flavor. It can be your main entree but is also excellent in smaller servings with cold-cuts and cold baked ham or beef if your diet allows.

1-1/2 ozs. Mozarella cheese
1-1/2 cups (8 ozs.) cooked noodles
1 cup ricotta cheese
1 tsp. Kosher or regular salt
1/2 tsp. instant minced onions

1 tsp. honey
1 egg, slightly beaten
1/2 cup milk
1/4 tsp. nutmeg
2 cups water

Cut cheese in very small cubes. Combine with noodles in medium bowl. Add ricotta, salt, onions, honey, egg, milk and nutmeg. Toss lightly to mix. Lightly oil a 1 quart aluminum pressure cooker mold or ring mold. Pour noodle mixture into it. Cover with foil and secure by tightly crimping around edges or tie with string. Place mold on rack in cooker. Add water. Cover and set control at 5. Cook 2-1/2 minutes after control jiggles. (For cookers having 15 pound setting only, decrease cooking time 1 minute.) Reduce pressure normally. Serve at once. Makes 4 servings.

NOODLES WITH CREAMED VEGETABLES

1 tsp. salt
2 qts. water
1 tbs. vegetable oil
1 pkg. (8 ozs.) noodles
2 tbs. margarine, melted
1 tbs. chopped ripe olives
1 tsp. chopped chives

2 tbs. toasted sesame seed
3/4 cup sour cream
1/2 cup toasted mixed nuts
vegetables, creamed or
    sprinkled with lemon juice
hard-cooked egg, grated

Bring salted water to rapid boil in uncovered cooker. Add vegetable oil. Reduce heat. Stir noodles in gradually. Cover cooker and set control at 5. Bring pressure up slowly to minimize frothing. Cook 4 minutes after control jiggles. (For cookers having 15 pound setting only, remove from heat as soon as control jiggles.) Reduce pressure at once by placing cooker under cold running water. Pour noodles into colander and let hot water run through them. Drain well and return to cooker. Stir in melted margarine and remaining ingredients. Toss to blend. Serve with your choice of creamed vegetables, topped with grated hard cooked egg, or with plain vegetables sprinkled with lemon juice. Makes 4 servings.

RICE CASSEROLE

1 cup long grain brown rice
1-1/2 cups water
1 tsp. salt
1 tsp. oil
2 cups water
1 cup mayonnaise
1 cup tomato juice

1 cup milk
1 green pepper, finely chopped
2-1/2 cups mushrooms
sweet vermouth or other wine
3/4 cup sliced, blanched almonds
   or water chestnuts

Combine rice, water and salt in oiled 1 quart mold. Place rack and water in cooker. Set rice on rack. Cover cooker and set control at 5. Cook 45 minutes after control jiggles. (For cookers having 15 pound setting only, decrease cooking time 20 to 27 minutes.) Reduce pressure at once by placing cooker under cold running water. Uncover cooker and remove mold and rack. Drain water from cooker. Transfer rice from mold to cooker. Stir in mayonnaise, tomato juice, milk and green pepper. Sauté mushrooms in a small amount of wine. Add to rice mixture. Turn heat to lowest setting and simmer 10 minutes, uncovered, until pepper is tender and all ingredients are well heated. Toss in almonds and serve. Makes 4 servings.

PEPPERS STUFFED WITH VEGETABLES

A good choice for main fare when you want to omit meat; a hearty vegetable when used to accompany meat.

4 green peppers
boiling water
2 tbs. margarine
1 tbs. flour
2/3 cup tomato juice
1/2 tsp. salt

1/8 tsp. freshly ground pepper
1/4 tsp. sweet basil
3/4 cup frozen corn
3/4 frozen, cut green beans
3/4 cup water

Wash peppers, remove stems, seeds and membranes. Pour boiling water over peppers and let stand 3 minutes. Drain thoroughly. Melt margarine in saucepan. Add flour and stir to blend. Pour in tomato juice, stirring constantly to give a velvety sauce. Add seasonings. Pour boiling water over vegetables and drain. Break vegetables into small pieces and add to sauce. Spoon in peppers. Add water to cooker. Make a "pie plate" from a double fold of heavy duty foil crimped at edges, and set in cooker. Place peppers on foil plate. Cover cooker and set control at 10. Cook 15 minutes after control jig-

gles. (For cookers having 15 pound setting only, decrease cooking time 3 minutes.) Reduce pressure normally 5 minutes, then place cooker under cold running water. Uncover and serve. Makes 4 servings.

Variations

Omit vegetables and substitute 3/4 pound lean ground beef and 1 small minced onion, browned in 1 tablespoon oil. Blend in 1/3 cup cooked rice. Omit sweet basil and use 1/4 teaspoon thyme.

Omit vegetables. Stuff peppers with 2 cups cooked, brown rice seasoned with sautéed onion bits and 2 teaspoons minced parsley.

Omit vegetables and use 1 cup cooked, flaked fish, 1/4 cup parboiled celery and 1/2 cup dry French bread crumbs. Increase tomato juice to 3/4 cup and omit basil. Instead spice with a dash of Tabasco sauce. Serve with lemon swirls.

STUFFED TURNIPS

In Lorna J. Sass' charming little cookbook, *To the Queen's Taste,* published by the Metropolitan Museum of Art, she tells about the inventiveness of Elizabethan cooks. In finding "containers" for their various fillings, vegetables such as carrots, cucumbers and turnips came into fashion. This recipe came from my Maine-born grandmother.

3 large white turnips, peeled
1 cup minced apples
2 tbs. raisins, minced fine
1 tbs. glacé mixed fruits, minced fine
2 hard-cooked eggs, grated
2 tbs. bread crumbs
1/8 tsp. salt
1/4 tsp. allspice
1 tbs. brown sugar

1 cup water
1/2 cup white table wine
1 tbs. margarine
6 *small* rosemary clusters
1/4 tsp. vinegar
1/8 tsp. mace, optional
12 pitted prunes, cooked
4 wedges cheddar or Colby cheese

Flatten turnips by slicing off tops and bottoms so they will stand on either end. Cut each turnip in half horizontally. Cut out a circle in each turnip, leaving a 1/8 inch rim.

Scoop until you have a small bowl effect. Sprinkle each lightly with salt. In a bowl combine apple, raisins, glace´ fruits, grated eggs, bread crumbs, salt, allspice and brown sugar. Divide mixture between scooped out turnips. In cooker bring water and wine to a gentle boil over low heat. Stir in margarine, vinegar, rosemary and mace. Place rack in cooker. Arrange stuffed turnips on rack and spoon a little liquid over each. Cover and set control at 15. Cook 5 minutes after control jiggles. Reduce pressure at once by placing cooker under cold running water. Serve while hot, spooning wine liquid over each. Garnish with prunes or other cooked dried fruits and wedges of cheese. Makes 3 to 4 servings.

VEGETABLE MELANGE

1 cauliflower, broken into flowerets
1 parsnip, quartered and cut lengthwise
4 medium carrots, scraped and cut into quarters, lengthwise
2 stalks broccoli, cut into flowerets; stems cut in 1/4 in. slices
1 cup green string beans, broken at ends and in half
1 scant tsp. salt
1/8 tsp. lemon pepper
3/4 cup water
3 tbs. browned margarine
lemon and cheese wedges

Wash and prepare vegetables as directed. Place rack in cooker and add water. Arrange vegetables on rack and sprinkle with salt. Cover and set control at 15. Cook 2-1/2 to 3 minutes after control jiggles. Reduce pressure at once by placing cooker under cold running water. Arrange vegetables on large serving platter and serve with browned margarine. Garnish with lemon wedges (for exciting flavor accent and added vitamin C) and cheese wedges for added protein.

WALNUT MOLD

Any nuts, plain or in combination, may be used in this recipe. Serve with fruit or carrot-apple-raisin salad and your favorite green vegetables.

1 cup walnuts, finely ground
2 cups whole grain bread crumbs
2 eggs, slightly beaten
1 tsp. savory
1 tsp. salt

1/8 tsp. white pepper, optional
2 cups hot milk
1-1/2 cups water
paprika

Mix together walnuts, bread crumbs, eggs and seasonings. Add milk, and stir to thoroughly blend. Spoon into lightly oiled pressure cooker mold and cover tightly with double fold aluminum foil crimped tightly around edges, or tied with string. Pour water into cooker and add rack. Set mold on rack. Cover cooker and set control at 5. Cook 5 minutes after control jiggles. (For cookers having 15 pound setting only, decrease cooking time 1-1/2 minutes.) Reduce pressure normally. Sprinkle with paprika, and set under broiler for 1 to 2 minutes to lightly brown top. Unmold and serve. Makes 4 servings.

Vegetables, A Vitamins Plus

Cooking fresh vegetables the pressure cooker way requires only about one-third the cooking time used by other methods. This conserves important vitamins and minerals and helps to preserve the natural color of vegetables.

Vegetables that have similar cooking times may be cooked together without a comingling of flavors. However, if you desire to keep the vegetables separate for serving, you may put each variety in an individual metal or ovenproof container. Place on rack in cooker and add indicated amount of water to bottom of cooker. Or make a container out of several thicknesses of aluminum foil and shape by pressing it over a pan or bowl. Containers should not be covered but cooking time needs to be slightly increased.

The fresh vegetable table which follows is used with permission of the Mirro Aluminum Company and gives you all the basics you need to know. It is, of course, only a guide because variation in age and size of vegetables will alter cooking times. The amount of water called for should be used whether cooking a panful or a cupful. Be sure to reduce pressure instantly to prevent overcooking.

In most instances you will not need to use the rack, but if you choose to, increase water by 1/4 cup.

119

FRESH VEGETABLE TABLE

Fresh Vegetable	Amount of Water 2-1/2 to 4 quarts	Pounds Pressure	Minutes to Cook After Control Jiggles
Artichoke	1 cup	15	15*
Asparagus	1/2 cup	15	2 — 2-1/2*
Beans, Green or Wax	1/2 cup	15	3*
Beans, Lima	1/2 cup	15	2*
Beets (sliced)	3/4 cup	15	6*
Beets (Small, whole)	3/4 cup	15	12*
Beets (large, whole)	1 cup	15	18*
Broccoli	1/2 cup	15	2-1/2*
Brussels Sprouts	3/4 cup	15	5*
Cabbage (shredded)	3/4 cup	15	3*
Cabbage (wedges)	3/4 cup	15	8*
Cabbage, Red (shredded)	3/4 cup	15	5*
Carrots (sliced)	1/4 cup	15	2-1/2*
Carrots (small, whole)	1/4 cup	15	4*
Cauliflower (flowerets)	1/2 cup	15	3*
Cauliflower (whole)	1 cup	15	6-8*
Celery	1/2 cup	15	5*
Celery Root	1/2 cup	15	5*
Corn (on the cob)	1 cup	15	5*
Corn (whole kernel)	1/2 cup	15	3*
Eggplant	1/2 cup	15	3*
Kale or Collards	1/2 cup	15	4-6*

Fresh Vegetables	Amount of Water 2-1/2 to 4 quarts	Pounds Pressure	Minutes to Cook After Control Jiggles
Kohlrabi	1/2 cup	15	4*
Okra	1/2 cup	15	3*
Onions (sliced)	1/2 cup	15	3*
Onions (whole, medium)	3/4 cup	15	7-10*
Parsnips (sliced)	1/2 cup	15	2*
Parsnips (halves)	3/4 cup	15	7*
Peas	1/2 cup	15	2*
Potatoes (sliced)	1 cup	15	2-1/2*
Potatoes (medium, cut in half)	1-1/2 cups	15	8*
Potatoes (medium, whole)	1-1/2 cups	15	12-15*
Potatoes, Sweet or Yams (quartered)	1 cup	15	6*
Potatoes, Sweet or Yams (halves)	1 cup	15	8-10*
Pumpkin	1-1/4 cups	15	8-10*
Rutabagas	3/4 cup	15	5*
Spinach, Swiss Chard or Other Greens	1/2 cup	15	1-1/2*
Squash, Acorn	3/4 cup	15	6-7*
Squash, Hubbard	3/4 cup	15	8-10*
Squash, Summer or Zucchini	3/4 cup	15	3-4*
Tomatoes	1/4 cup	15	2-1/2*
Turnips	3/4 cup	15	5*

*Reduce pressure instantly by placing under cold running water.

FROZEN VEGETABLES TABLE

Vegetable	Amount of Water	Pounds Pressure	Minutes to Cook After Control Jiggles
Asparagus Spears	1/2 cup	15	2*
Asparagus Cuts	1/2 cup	15	2-1/2*
Broccoli	1/2 cup	15	3*
Broccoli Cuts	1/2 cup	15	2*
Brussels Sprouts	1/2 cup	15	2-1/2*
Cauliflower	1/2 cup	15	2*
Corn, whole kernel	1/2 cup	15	1*
Corn on the Cob	1/2 cup	15	2*
Green Beans, cut	1/2 cup	15	3*
Green Beans, French style	1/2 cup	15	1*
Green Peas	1/2 cup	15	1*
Lima Beans, small	1/2 cup	15	2-1/2*
Lima Beans, large	1/2 cup	15	4*
Mixed Vegetables	1/2 cup	15	2*
Peas and Carrots	1/2 cup	15	2*
Spinach	1/2 cup	15	1*
Wax Beans	1/2 cup	15	3*

*Reduce pressure instantly by placing cooker under cold running water.

DRIED BEANS & LENTILS TABLE

Used with permission of Mirro Aluminum Company

Vegetable	Water for 1 Cup Dried Beans or Lentils	Pounds of Pressure	Minutes to Cook After Control Jiggles
Black Eyed Peas	1-1/2 cups	15	10*
Kidney Beans	2 cups	15	30*
Lentils	2 cups	15	20*
Lima Beans, large	2 cups	15	30*
Lima Beans, small	2 cups	15	25*
Navy Beans	2 cups	15	30*
Pea Beans	2 cups	15	20*
Pinto Beans	2 cups	15	10*
Soy Beans	2 cups	15	35*

Soak all dried beans or lentils overnight in water to cover. Drain; add necessary water and 1 tablespoon vegetable oil to prevent frothing. Don't overload cooker. Never fill more than 2/3 to 3/4 full with at least 1-1/4 inches space between rim of cooker and top of liquid.

*Reduce pressure normally 5 minutes then place under cold, running water.

ARTICHOKES CALIFORNIA

One of the real delicacies among the vegetable family, this edible thistle is an exotic addition to any dinner as a hot vegetable or cold as a salad or hors d'oeuvre. But to achieve its special texture and taste, you must give it some tender ministrations. It means preparing it so that its special flavor is brought to its zenith. This requires a little more salt than for most vegetables. Happily, with a pressure cooker, there is no problem about the length of cooking — the artichoke is cooked just long enough so that its leaves are delicate and soft.

4 medium artichokes
2 tsp. dehydrated onion flakes
1-1/4 cup warm water
2 tsp. salt
1 tbs. vegetable oil
1 tsp. minced rosemary (optional)

Remove lower outer leaves of artichokes. With scissors snip off sharp tips from leaves. Cut stems so artichokes will sit flat in cooker. Wash thoroughly under cold

water. Place in cooker. Scatter onion flakes among leaves of each choke. Blend warm water, salt and oil, and stir until salt is dissolved. Pour this mixture evenly over artichokes letting most of it settle on bottom of pan. Cover and set control at 15. Cook 15 minutes after control jiggles. Reduce pressure at once by placing cooker under cold running water. Serve hot or cold with mayonnaise, Hurry-Up Hollandaise (page 135) or Mustard Sauce (page 147). Makes 4 servings.

ASPARAGUS WITH HERBS AND THINGS

Do not thaw frozen asparagus before pressure cooking. Time all vegetables carefully after control jiggles because it is important not to overcook them. Season vegetables before or after cooking. Point up flavor with a little lemon juice, as desired.

1/4 cup onion, diced
1 green pepper, chopped fine
1/2 tsp. salt
1/8 tsp. white pepper
1/2 cup water

2 pkgs. (10 ozs. ea.) frozen asparagus spears
1 tbs. lemon juice
1 tbs. pimiento, diced small
1/2 tsp. tarragon, crumbled
1 tbs. parlsey, minced

Put onion, green pepper, salt, pepper and water in cooker and bring to a boil. Reduce heat and add asparagus. Cover and set control at 15. Cook 2 to 2-1/2 minutes after control jiggles. Reduce pressure at once by placing cooker under cold running water. Remove and sprinkle with lemon juice. Garnish with pimiento, tarragon and parsley. Makes 4 to 6 servings.

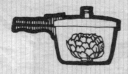

GREEN BEANS WITH WATER CHESTNUTS

1 lb. fresh green or wax beans
1/2 cup water
1/2 tsp. salt
1 can (8 ozs.) water chestnuts, sliced

Wash beans thoroughly and remove ends. Leave whole or slice on diagonal or French cut. Add water, salt and beans to cooker. Cover and set control at 15. Cook 3 minutes for whole; 2 minutes for diagonally or French cut, after control jiggles. Reduce pressure at once by placing cooker under cold running water. Remove cover and stir in water chestnuts. Set cooker, uncovered, over low heat for 1 minute. Serve at once. Makes 4 servings.

Variation

One-half cup toasted almonds may be substituted for water chestnuts. Add just before serving.

DILLED BEANS, SOUTHERN STYLE

1 cup *plus* 2 tbs. water
1 beef bouillon cube
2 tbs. onion, finely chopped
1/2 tsp. dill seed
2 pkgs. (9 ozs. ea.) frozen green beans

Bring water to boil in cooker over medium heat. Add bouillon and dissolve. Add onion and simmer 2 minutes. Stir in dill seed and beans. Cover and set control at 15. Cook 1 to 3 minutes (cut green beans, 3 minutes; French style green beans, 1 minute) after control jiggles. Reduce pressure at once by placing cooker under cold running water. Drain and save liquid. Keep beans warm while preparing sauce. Makes 6 servings.

Always nudge control with long handled fork before removing. If steam sizzles cooker is not ready to be opened.

Southern Style Sauce

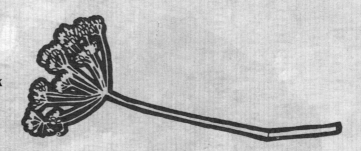

1/4 cup margarine
1/4 cup flour
1-1/2 cups bean liquid plus milk
1 tsp. salt
1/8 tsp. cayenne
2 tbs. vinegar

Melt margarine in saucepan. Blend in flour. Gradually add liquid and cook, stirring, until thickened. Add seasonings. Simmer 5 minutes, stirring constantly. Pour over beans. Reheat 1 minute. Makes 1-1/2 cups sauce.

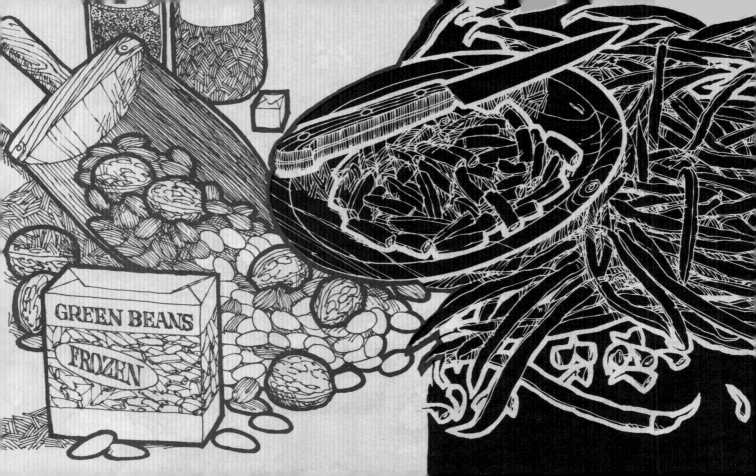

GREEN BEANS

FROZEN

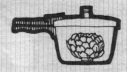

RIVIERA GREEN BEANS

1/2 cup water
1 beef bouillon cube
1 pkg. (9 ozs.) frozen, cut green beans
1/2 tsp. salt
1 tbs. red wine vinegar
1 tsp. paprika
1 tbs. cornstarch
1 tbs. water
1/8 tsp. garlic salt
1/2 cup chopped walnuts,
    blanched almonds or pecans

Pour water into cooker. Add bouillon cube, green beans and salt. Cover and set control at 15. Cook 3 minutes after control jiggles. Reduce pressure at once by setting cooker under cold running water. In small saucepan blend vinegar, paprika, cornstarch, water and garlic salt. Cook over low heat, stirring to keep smooth. When slightly thickened, stir in nuts and pour over green beans. Serve at once. Makes 4 servings.

"STIR-FRY" BEAN SPROUTS

1-1/2 tbs. vegetable oil
1/4 lb. mushrooms
2 stalks celery, cut into bite-size pieces
1 lb. bean sprouts
1/2 tsp. salt

1 tbs. soy sauce, optional
1/8 tsp. marjoram
1/8 tsp. sweet basil
1/2 cup water
1 tbs. lemon juice

Heat oil in cooker. Add mushrooms and celery and lightly sauté. Wash bean sprouts, drain well and add to mushrooms. Stir in remaining ingredients, except lemon juice. Cover and set control at 15. Cook 1 minutes after control jiggles. Reduce pressure at once by placing cooker under cold running water. Uncover. Drain vegetables and sprinkle with lemon juice. Makes 4 servings.

Note: Other vegetable combinations may be substituted for mushrooms and celery. Chopped nuts or sliced water chestnuts are a nice addition.

RUSSIAN BEETS

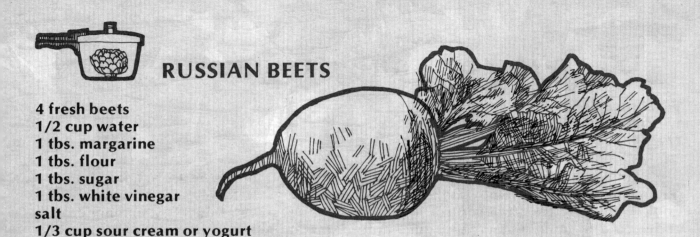

4 fresh beets
1/2 cup water
1 tbs. margarine
1 tbs. flour
1 tbs. sugar
1 tbs. white vinegar
salt
1/3 cup sour cream or yogurt

Scrub beets thoroughly. Remove all but 3 inches of tops and leave roots on. Place in cooker with water. Cover and set control at 15. Cook 10 to 18 minutes, depending upon age and size of beets, after control jiggles. Reduce pressure at once by placing cooker under cold running water. Drain and peel beets. Melt margarine in cooker. Blend in flour and sugar. Stir in vinegar and salt to taste. Slice or grate beets into vinegar mixture. Simmer over low heat one minute. Add sour cream and simmer 1 minute more until heated. Makes 4 servings.

BROCCOLI WITH HURRY-UP HOLLANDAISE ·

1 lb. broccoli
1/2 cup water
1/2 tsp. salt

   Remove large outer leaves of broccoli and cut off tough part of stalks. Cut into serving pieces and drop into cooker. Pour in water and salt. Cover and set control at 15. Cook 2-1/2 minutes after control jiggles. Reduce pressure at once by placing cooker under cold running water. Serve on warm plates topped with Hurry-Up Hollandaise. Makes 4 generous servings.

Hurry-Up Hollandaise

I gave it this name because it is made in a hurry and must be used in a hurry! Do not let stand or it may separate.

4 egg yolks
2 tbs. lemon juice
1/8 tsp., scant, cayenne
1/4 tsp. salt
2/3 cup margarine, heated to bubbling stage

Place first 4 ingredients in blender container. Cover and blend at high speed 3 seconds. Remove cover and with blender running, pour in melted margarine. By time all is poured in (about 1/2 minute), the sauce should be slightly thickened and ready to serve *at once* over broccoli. Freeze any leftover sauce and reheat over hot water. Makes about 1 cup.

135

GERMAN STYLE RED CABBAGE

1 small head red cabbage
2 red apples, cored but not peeled
2 tbs. vegetable oil
1/2 tsp. salt
1/8 tsp. black pepper

3/4 cup water
3 tbs. cider vinegar
1 tsp. sugar
1 tbs. flour
1/4 tsp. caraway seed, optional

Remove outer leaves of cabbage and discard. Quarter, core and shred cabbage into cooker. Slice unpeeled apples and add to cabbage. Add oil, salt and pepper. Pour in water. Cover and set control at 15. Cook 5 minutes after control jiggles. Reduce pressure at once by placing cooker under cold running water. Uncover and drain into heated serving dish. Mix vinegar, sugar and flour and caraway seed. Stir in liquid from cooker. Return to cooker and heat until mixture thickens, stirring constantly to avoid lumping. Add cabbage and reheat. Serve at once. Makes 4 servings.

When in doubt about amount of liquid to use in adapting your own recipes, never use less, but you can use more as long as it doesn't exceed the limit specified.

GLAZED CARROTS

4 carrots, scrubbed
1/2 cup water
1/2 tsp. salt
1/3 cup melted margarine
1/3 cup brown sugar
paprika

Slice carrots in half, lengthwise and drop into cooker. Add salted water. Cover and set control at 15. Cook 4 minutes after control jiggles. Reduce pressure at once by placing cooker under cold running water. Drain and skin carrots. Dip in margarine, then roll in brown sugar and sprinkle with paprika. Return to cooker and cook over medium heat, uncovered, until they develop a good glaze. Baste a time or two while glazing is in progress. Makes 4 servings.

Because they are extremely frothy and will clog the vent, never cook applesauce, rhubarb or cranberries in a pressure cooker.

137

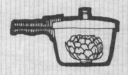

CARROT-PARSNIP PATTIES

A favorite of my father's, these patties were served in my childhood with roast leg of lamb or lamb chops. But they are equally good with beef or pork.

1 cup sliced carrots
1 cup sliced parsnips
1/2 cup water
1/2 tsp. salt

1 tbs. flour or bread crumbs
1/8 tsp. white pepper
1 tsp. cut-up chives
bacon drippings

Place carrots and parsnips in cooker. Add water and salt. Cover and set control at 15. Cook 2-1/2 minutes after control jiggles. Reduce pressure at once by placing cooker under cold running water. Drain vegetables and remove from cooker. Mash and blend in remaining ingredients except bacon drippings. Shape into 4 patties, adding a little more flour if patties are overly moist. Heat bacon drippings in cooker. Brown patties, uncovered, until golden on each side. Serve on warm plates. Makes 4 patties.

CELERY-CARROT MIX

4 stalks young celery
8 small whole carrots
1/2 cup water
1/2 tsp. salt
1/8 tsp. (scant) sugar
lemon juice
1/2 tsp. margarine
1 tbs. chopped parsley

Wash and string celery stalks, then cut into strips. Place in cooker. Wash and scrape carrots. Add to celery. Pour in salted water. Cover and set control at 15. Cook 4 minutes after control jiggles. Reduce pressure at once by placing cooker under cold running water. Uncover and stir in remaining ingredients. The carrots give this combination dish enough color and the celery chewiness to serve with meats, or bland dishes such as veal and fish. Makes 4 servings.

 # CHINESE PEA PODS WITH WATER CHESTNUTS

2 pkgs. (6 ozs. ea.) frozen Chinese pea pods
    or 1 lb. fresh pea pods
1/2 cup water
1/8 tsp. grated nutmeg
1/2 can (8 ozs.) peeled water chestnuts, sliced
soy sauce

Break ends from pea pods if necessary. Place pods in cooker. Add water and cover. Set control at 15. Cook 1 minutes after control jiggles. Reduce pressure at once by placing cooker under cold running water. Stir in sliced water chestnuts and about 1-1/2 teaspoons soy sauce. Blend and serve.

Variation

Omit sliced water chestnuts, and substitute 2 tablespoons chopped green onions. Omit nutmeg and use 1/2 teaspoon sugar. Makes 4 servings.

CORN CONFETTI

Frozen corn on the cob is the one frozen vegetable that must be completely thawed before cooking under pressure.

1 pkg. (10 ozs.) frozen corn on the cob
1/2 cup water
1/2 tsp. salt
melted margarine
1/4 green pepper, minced
1 jar (1 oz.) pimiento, cut into very small pieces
1/8 tsp. (scant) lemon pepper

Remove corn from package and break into halves or thirds, depending upon size of ear. Let thaw completely. Then drop into cooker with salted water. Cover and set control at 15. Cook 5 minutes after control jiggles. Reduce pressure at once by placing cooker under cold running water. Drain and cut corn from cob. Return to cooker and combine with remaining ingredients. Simmer over low heat 7 minutes. Serve with beef, pork, veal or poultry. Makes 4 servings.

EGGPLANT, ITALIAN STYLE

2 (about 1 lb. ea.) eggplants
flour
2 eggs, beaten slightly
6 tbs. olive oil
4 tbs. margarine
1 onion, chopped small

3/4 cup water
1-1/2 cups tomato juice
1/8 tsp. sweet basil
1 tsp. salt
1/3 cup dry bread crumbs
Parmesan cheese

Wash and slice eggplant into 1/2-inch slices. Roll each slice in flour, then dip into eggs. Brown in hot oil in cooker. Remove from cooker. Add margarine as needed to saute onions. Cook 5 minutes. Remove from cooker. Pour water into cooker and add rack. Make a fluted double thickness foil container. Place on rack. Layer eggplant and onions into it. Combine tomato juice, sweet basil and salt. Pour over eggplant mixture. Sprinkle with bread crumbs. Top with Parmesan cheese. Cover and set control at 15. Cook 1 minute after control jiggles. Reduce pressure at once by placing cooker under cold running water. Set eggplant on cookie sheet and broil to lightly brown cheese. Makes 4 servings.

143

GLAZED ONIONS

1 lb. white, pearl onions
1/2 cup water
1/2 tsp. salt
2 tbs. margarine
4 tbs. sugar
1/4 tsp. grated nutmeg

Peel onions and put into cooker with water and salt. Cover and set control at 15. Cook 7 minutes after control jiggles. Reduce pressure at once by placing cooker under cold running water. Drain onions and turn into skillet in which margarine has been melted. Sprinkle with sugar and nutmeg, and cook over medium heat until onions are golden and glazed. Makes 4 servings.

Cover should never be forced off. Cool cooker until cover can be easily removed.

OKRA STEW, LOUISIANA STYLE

2 tbs. vegetable oil
1 onion, peeled and sliced thin
1/2 green pepper, diced
1 cup tomatoes
1/3 cup corn kernels

1 cup sliced okra
1/2 tsp. salt
1/4 tsp. freshly ground pepper
1/4 tsp. file´powder
1/2 cup water

Heat oil in cooker. Saute´ onion. Add green pepper and cook 1 minute. Stir in tomatoes, corn, okra and seasonings. Pour water over all and cover. Set control at 15. Cook 3 minutes after control jiggles. Reduce pressure at once by placing cooker under cold running water. Makes 4 servings.

Note: If you use canned okra instead of fresh, do not discard muciliaginous substance, but let it become part of stew.

PEAS AND NEW POTATOES IN CREAM SAUCE

This recipe heralds spring when fresh peas and new potatoes are at their peak of goodness. Perfect with roast beef, spring lamb, pork or ham.

1 cup Cream Sauce, page 147
4 small new potatoes
1-1/2 lbs. peas, shelled
salt
1 cup water
paprika

Prepare sauce as directed, using half-and-half. Cover with plastic wrap pressed against the surface, and keep warm while potatoes and peas cook. Scrub potatoes and cut in quarters. Place on rack in cooker. Add peas and salt. Pour in water. Cover and set control at 15. Cook 2-1/2 minutes after control jiggles. Reduce pressure at once by placing cooker under cold running water. Drain and pour cream sauce over potatoes and peas. Stir gently to mix. Simmer until thoroughly heated. Sprinkle with paprika. Makes 4 servings.

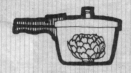

Cream Sauce

2 tbs. margarine
2 tbs. flour
1 cup heated half-and-half or milk
1/4 tsp. salt
freshly ground white pepper
nutmeg, optional

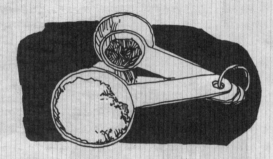

   Melt margarine in heavy saucepan over medium heat. (Do not let brown.) Add flour and stir to blend, preferably using a wire whisk. Add half-and-half all at once while stirring. When mixture bubbles it will thicken automatically Continue to cook, stirring, 5 minutes to cook flour. Add seasonings. Makes 1 cup.
   For Mustard Sauce: Combine 1 teaspoon dry mustard with flour when making Cream Sauce.

SURPRISE SWEET POTATOES

3 large or 4 medium sweet
   potatoes or yams
1 cup water
2 tbs. margarine

1/2 cup or more orange juice
3/4 cup well drained crushed pineapple
salt

Wash, peel and quarter sweet potatoes. Place on rack in cooker with water. Cover and set control at 15. Cook 6 minutes after control jiggles. Reduce pressure at once by placing cooker under cold running water. Remove cover and drain potatoes. Add margarine and mash. Stir in orange juice and blend, then add pineapple. Lightly salt and taste. Add more juice or pineapple, if needed to give desired consistency. Makes 4 servings.

Variation

Add 2 tablespoons flour to potato-fruit mix and form into 3-inch balls. Dip in beaten egg and roll in 1 cup crumbled corn flakes. Deep fry until golden. Delicious with turkey and trimmings.

GOLDEN RISOTTO

The best way to pressure cook rice is in an uncovered mold or pan set on rack in cooker. See Rice Table, page 150.

2 tbs. vegetable oil	1 cup long grain brown rice	1 cup cut-up ham
1/2 cup onions, chopped	1/8 tsp. saffron (powder)	1 can (4 ozs.) mushrooms
2 cups bouillon	1 cup diced cooked chicken	1/4 cup Parmesan cheese

Heat oil in cooker over medium heat. Add onions and sauté until lightly brown. Add hot bouillon and stir to blend. Pour rice into oiled mold. Add hot bouillon mixture. Place rack and 2 cups water in cooker. Set mold on rack. Cover and set control at 5. Cook 45 minutes after control jiggles. (For cookers having 15 pound setting only, decrease cooking time 20 to 27 minutes.) Reduce pressure at once by placing cooker under cold running water. Remove rice, rack and water from cooker. Pour rice into cooker. Add remaining ingredients. Correct seasoning. (Bouillons vary in saltiness so you will have to taste to know if additional salt is needed.) Stir to blend and heat slowly to serving temperature. Serve at once. Makes 4 to 6 servings.

RICE TABLE

According to Mirro-Matic's model booklet, *Speed Pressure Cooker and Canner*, the best way to pressure cook rice is in an uncovered pressure cooker mold or pan set on rack in cooker. The following table is used with the permission of the Mirror Aluminum Company.

	Rice	Water in Cups	Salt	Minutes to Cook After Control Jiggles	Pounds Pressure
Long grain rice	1 cup	1-1/2	1 tsp.	15	5
(regular or converted)				5-7	15
Long grain brown rice	1/2 cup	1-1/2	1/2 tsp.	45	5
(regular)				18-25	15
Wild rice	1/2 cup	1-1/4	1/2 tsp.	50	5
				20	15

1. Place rice, water and salt in oiled 1-quart, pressure cooker mold.
2. Place on rack in cooker. Add 2 cups water to cooker.
3. Cover, set control at 5 and cook.
4. Reduce pressure instantly by placing cooker under cold running water. Remove rice from mold.

PASTA TABLE

Adapted from material furnished by Mirro Aluminum Company.

	Amount of Pasta	Amount of Water	Minutes to Cook	Pressure
Macaroni	2 cups	2 quarts	6*	5
	(8 ozs.)		6*	15
Noodles	2 cups	2 quarts	4*	5
	(6-2/3 ozs.)		4*	15
Spaghetti	2-1/2 cups	2 quarts	8*	5
	(8 ozs.)		8*	15

In preparing one of the above always bring salted water to rapid boil in cooker. Add pasta and 1 tablespoon vegetable oil. Stir and reduce heat. Cover and set control. Count cooking time when control begins to jiggle. Never fill cooker more than 2/3 to 3/4 full, and always allow 1-1/4 inch space between rim of cooker and top of liquid.

*Reduce pressure at once by placing cooker under cold running water. Then place pasta in colander, run hot water over it and drain well.

Custards And Fruit Desserts

Custards and dried or fresh fruit cooked in your pressure cooker are bound to bring you raves. Delicate in texture and flavor, custards are a bonus ending to any carefully prepared meal. And they invite many variations. Several are given in this section as well as for the special baby custard on page 170 of the baby section.

Custards and steamed puddings may be made in individual or 1-quart aluminum molds as directed. If glass or ceramic containers are used, extend cooking time to 10 minutes after control jiggles at 5 pounds pressure. If you are using a cooker with 15 pound setting only, reduce cooking time 3 minutes. Let cool normally to reduce pressure.

You may find occasional condensation on top of custards after removing them from cooker. Simply spoon off any liquid or absorb with a paper towel. Sprinkle tops with nutmeg or seasoning of your choice.

When your dessert choice includes dried fruit, be sure to allow time to rehydrate. By soaking selected fruit, water absorption will erase the so-called wrinkles of dried fruit. A general guide is to soak 1 cup dried fruit in 1-1/2 cups hot water for at least 1 hour. When you cook rehydrated fruit at 15 pounds pressure, allow 2 cups water for each pound dried fruit. (See table on page 157 for additional information.)

CUSTARD

This delicious custard developed by Mirro-Matic (Mirro Aluminum Company) is so perfect I see no reason to change it and am grateful for their permission to use it here.

2 eggs
2 tbs. sugar (or honey, my addition)
1 tsp. pure vanilla extract
dash salt

2 cups hot, not boiled, milk
1/2 cup water
nutmeg

Beat eggs slightly in medium bowl. Add sugar, vanilla, salt and hot milk. Beat lightly to blend. Pour custard into 4 individual, lightly oiled aluminum custard cups. Place rack in cooker and pour in water. Set custards on rack. Cover and set control at 5. Cook exactly 1 minute after control jiggles. (For cookers having 15 pound setting only, remove from heat as soon as control jiggles.) Remove cooker from heat and reduce pressure normally. Sprinkle custards with nutmeg. Chill before serving. Makes 4 servings.

Note: If glass or ceramic custard cups are used, increase cooking time to 2-1/2 minutes after control jiggles for 5 pound setting. For 15 pound setting, cook 1 minute after control jiggles.

Variations

Omit vanilla and substitute a scant 1/8 teaspoon Angostura bitters.

Omit nutmeg and serve with Raspberry Sauce.

To make custard in a 1-quart aluminum mold, use 3 cups hot milk, 3 eggs, 3 table-spoons sugar and 1-1/2 teaspoons vanilla extract. Increase water in cooker to 1 cup and cook 10 minutes after control jiggles. (For cookers having 15 pound setting only, decrease cooking time 6 minutes.) Reduce pressure normally. If a glass or ceramic mold is used cook custards 15 minutes, and decrease cooking time 3 minutes for 15 pound setting.

Raspberry Sauce — Hull, wash and sieve 1 basket raspberries. Add about 1/2 cup sugar (or to taste) and purée in food processor or blender, or beat 10 minutes with electric hand beater. Sugar should be completely dissolved and the purée quite thick. Add 2 tablespoons Kirsch or Cognac. (If frozen berries are used, thaw and drain thoroughly. Force through a sieve and beat in some of their syrup to thin. Add liqueur as above.)

DEEP SOUTH PRALINE CUSTARD

1/4 cup margarine
1/2 cup brown sugar
1/2 cup finely cut walnuts or pecans
3 eggs
3 tbs. sugar

1/2 tsp. salt
1 tsp. sherry
3 cups hot, not boiled, milk
1 cup water

Melt margarine in bottom of an aluminum pie plate. Stir in sugar and bake in 350°F. oven 5 minutes. Add nuts and bake 3 minutes longer. Praline mixture should bubble and boil. Remove from oven and quickly pour into a lightly oiled, 1-quart aluminum mold. Tip mold to coat sides with praline mixture. Set aside while making custard. Beat eggs slightly in medium bowl. Add sugar, salt, sherry and hot milk. Beat lightly to blend. Pour into mold over praline mixture. Place rack in cooker and pour in water. Set mold on rack. Cover and set control at 5. Cook 10 minutes after control jiggles. (For cookers having 15 pound setting only, decrease cooking time 6 minutes.) Remove cooker from heat and reduce pressure normally. Chill thoroughly before serving. Makes 6 servings.

I am indebted to Mirro-Matic (Mirro Aluminum Company) for permission to use the following:

TABLE — DRIED FRUITS

Fruit	Amount of Water Per 1 Pound of Fruit	Pounds Pressure	Minutes to Cook After Control Jiggles
Apples	2 cups	15	2*
Apricots	2 cups	15	2*
Figs	2 cups	15	6*
Peaches	2 cups	15	4*
Pears	2 cups	15	4*
Prunes	2 cups	15	5-6*
Raisins	1 cup	15	5*

*Reduce pressure at once by placing cooker under cold running water or in pan of cold water.

HOT FRUIT COMPOTE

1 pkg. (8 ozs.) mixed dried fruits
1-1/2 cups hot water
1/4 cup sherry

1 Comice pear, optional
garnish

Wash fruit and place in cooker. Cover with hot, not boiling water, and sherry. Soak until soft, with most of wrinkles eliminated (about 40 to 60 minutes). Drain soaking liquid into measuring cup and add water to make 2 cups. Pour into cooker. Add washed, peeled and cup-up pear. Cover and set control at 15. Cook 3 to 6 minutes, depending upon combinations of fruits, after control jiggles. Reduce pressure at once by placing cooker under cold running water. Uncover and taste. Add a little honey if a sweeter melange is desired. Spoon into individual compotes. Garnish each with maraschino cherry, lychee nut or sprig of mint. Marke 4 servings.

Variation

Omit wine and use 4 drops Angostura bitters.

DRIED PEACH MELBA SUPREME

1 lb. dried peaches
hot water
2 tbs. sugar
2 slices lemon
Angostura bitters
1 basket fresh raspberries
    or 1 pkg. (10 ozs.) frozen raspberries
whipped cream or ice cream

Cover peaches with hot water and soak 30 to 60 minutes to rehydrate and un-wrinkle. Spoon peaches into cooker and measure liquid. Add water, as necessary, to make 2 cups. Top with sliced lemon. Cover and set control at 15. Cook 4 minutes after control jiggles. Reduce pressure at once by placing cooker under cold running water. Uncover and sprinkle 4 drops Angostura bitters onto fruit. Spoon 1 or more peaches into each serving dish. Fill cavities with raspberries. Top with flavored whipped cream or ice cream. Makes about 6 servings.

159

CRANBERRY-APPLE CRISP

1 cup dried apples
   or 2 cups peeled and sliced apples
1-1/2 tsp. lemon juice
3/4 cup quick cooking oats
1/3 cup flour

1/2 cup dark brown sugar
1/4 tsp. salt
1 tsp. cinnamon
1/3 cup melted margarine
1 can whole cranberry sauce

If using dried apples soak for 1 hour. Sprinkle apples with lemon juice. Combine oats, flour, brown sugar, cinnamon, salt and margarine. Place layer of apples on bottom of lightly oiled pressure cooker mold or dish that will fit loosely on rack in cooker. Top with half of oats mixture. Spread cranberry sauce over this. Sprinkle remaining oats mixture over cranberries. Cover mold or bowl with double fold of aluminum foil and secure. Place on rack in cooker. Add 2 cups water. Cover and set control at 5. Cook for 20 minutes after control jiggles. (For cookers having 15 pound setting only, decrease cooking time 3 minutes.) Reduce pressure at once by placing cooker under cold running water. If crisp topping is desired place under broiler 1 minute. Serve hot or cold with cream or a dollop of sour cream. Makes 4 to 5 servings.

GRANDMOTHER'S FANCY APPLE PUDDING

This old fashioned dessert is especially good served with Soft Custard Sauce (page 163) or a scoop of vanilla ice cream.

2 cups cooked dried apples
1-1/2 slices bread
margarine
2 tbs. brown sugar

1/2 tsp. caraway seed
1/2 tsp. vanilla extract
2-1/2 cups water

Prepare dried apples in cooker according to chart on page 157. Measure 2 cups cooked apples into oiled 1-quart aluminum mold or earthenware dish. Trim crusts from bread and spread with margarine. Cut in triangles. Sprinkle half of brown sugar and caraway over apples. Fit bread triangles over apples and use remaining sugar and caraway on top of bread. Sprinkle vanilla over all. Add water and rack to cooker. Place mold on rack. Cover and set control at 5. Cook 2 minutes after control jiggles. (For cookers having 15 pound setting only, decrease cooking time 1/2 minute.) Reduce pressure at once by placing cooker under cold running water. Remove mold from cooker and set under broiler for 1 minute to lightly brown. Makes 4 servings.

OLD FASHIONED PRUNE WHIP
WITH CUSTARD SAUCE

1-1/2 cups pitted prunes
water
1/2 tsp. freshly ground nutmeg
2 tsp. lemon juice
3 egg whites
1/8 tsp., scant, salt
1/4 cup sugar

Place prunes in a large bowl. Cover with water. Let stand 1 hour or more. Using a slotted spoon transfer prunes to cooker. Measure liquid and add enough water to make 2 cups. Pour over prunes. Cover and set control at 5. Cook 5 to 6 minutes after control jiggles. (For cookers having 15 pound pressure setting only, decrease cooking time 2 minutes.) Reduce pressure instantly by placing cooker under cold running water. Uncover, and add nutmeg. Purée prunes in blender, food mill or food processor. Add lemon juice. Beat egg whites with salt until frothy. Gradually beat in sugar until peaks stand soft yet firm. Add prune purée, 1/4 cup at a time, beating thoroughly. If you use a mixer for this, beat at high speed. Bake in unbuttered pudding dish in 300°F. oven 45

minutes or until firm to touch. Chill well. Serve with Soft Custard Sauce. Makes 4 to 6 servings.

Soft Custard Sauce

3 egg yolks
1 egg
1/3 cup sugar or honey
dash salt
2 cups hot, not boiled milk
nutmeg

Beat eggs in top of double boiler until well blended. Add sugar, salt and milk. Cook over hot water, stirring constantly until mixture coats a metal spoon. Pour into a small bowl. Refrigerate, covered, until chilled.

STEAMED PERSIMMON PUDDING

1 cup flour
1-1/2 tsp. baking soda
1/4 tsp. salt
1/2 tsp. cinnamon
1/2 cup dried bread crumbs
1/3 cup light brown sugar
1 cup persimmon pulp
1 egg, slightly beaten
2 tbs. melted margarine
1/2 cup milk
2 cups water

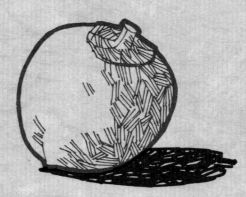

Sift flour, baking soda, salt and cinnamon into medium mixing bowl. Add crumbs, brown sugar, persimmon, egg, melted margarine and milk. Mix well. Pour mixture into lightly oiled, 1-quart aluminum mold. Cover with a "bonnet" or tent of double fold foil which will allow for expansion during cooking. Crimp edges and tie with string. Place rack in cooker and pour in water. Set mold on rack. Cover and allow steam to flow from

vent, without control, for 30 minutes. Then set control at 5 and cook 60 minutes after control jiggles. (For cookers having 15 pound setting only, decrease cooking time 15 minutes.) Reduce pressure at once by placing cooker under cold running water. Serve warm with hard sauce. Makes 12 servings.

Hard Sauce—In mixing bowl, cream 1/2 cup softened sweet butter and 1 cup confectioners' sugar together well. Add 2 tablespoons brandy or rum, a few drops at a time. Beat until fluffy. Sprinkle with nutmeg. Makes 1 cup.

When using a covered mold on the rack, add 1 teaspoon vinegar or 1/2 teaspoon cream of tartar to water under rack to prevent cooker from discoloring.

Something For Baby Too

Can your pressure cooker produce foods of high nutritive value for your baby? The answer is an unqualified *yes*. Pressure cooked foods retain more health giving vitamins and minerals than foods cooked by any other method. Rapid rise in temperature when cooking under steam halts certain undesirable enzymatic reactions from taking place which affect color, flavor and texture of foods.

One enzyme present in plant tissue is harmful to vitamin C. Rates at which enzymatic reactions affect food accelerate as temperature rises until the enzyme is destroyed. Thus the swift rise in temperature destroys the unwanted enzymatic reaction instantly, before it can affect food appreciably, according to Gretchen Ziesmer, Mirro Home Economist, Mirro Aluminum Company.

Another cooker boon to the additive-conscious parent is that you can cook exactly what you want, without any added ingredients you don't want in baby food. And your pressure cooker tenderizes protein foods naturally without chemical additives. The process used is the same as in commerical production of baby food.

You can count on your cooker to give maximum nutritive value to baby foods, better texture, color and flavor and will save you time and effort in the kitchen, cut down on utility bills, and cook baby food in about 1/3 less time than required by conventional methods.

Perhaps a few tips slanted to your special interest will help you on your way to better food for baby, the pressure cooker way.

1. Select fresh foods whenever possible. Remember that the cooked product can be no better than what you put into the cooker.

2. Store fresh foods promptly after purchase.

3. Foods that are to be pureed for baby should be cooked about half again as long as those prepared for older children and adults. After cooking, strain, blend or puree in food processor.

4. Cook whatever amount of food you wish, serving it fresh to baby the day of preparation. Freeze any remaining amount in ice trays or individual covered containers. In this way you can keep food costs down to a minimum just by preparing in-season foods for out-of-season use.

5. Do not save any uneaten food in baby dish. Throw out, as bacteria can quickly accumulate when saliva on feeding spoon mixes with food.

6. Rehydrate your dried foods for soups and stews for puree for baby.

7. Do not add salt to baby foods unless your baby is on a vegetarian diet. In this

case, with a higher carbohydrate-potassium diet, you'll have to add salt, but the amount should be determined by your physician or nutritionist, according to your baby's special needs.

8. Omit sugar when cooking fruits for purée. When you do add a sweetener in the latter part of the first year, use only half as much as you would for an adult serving, substituting a *little* honey or light brown sugar, as allowed. *Remember that all fruits, except bananas, must be cooked before straining.*

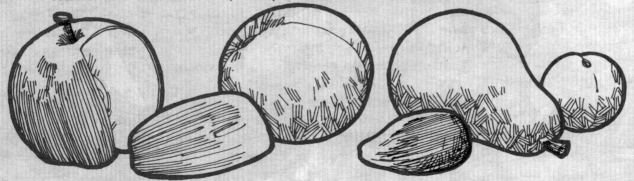

PLAIN CUSTARD

Simple and quick to make, this is bound to please any baby and is suitable after eggs have been added to diet.

1 cup milk

1 egg, room temperature

1 tsp. honey, optional after 6 months

1/2 cup water

Heat milk but do not boil. Beat egg slightly and stir in honey and milk. Pour into individual aluminum or oven-safe custard cups.* Place rack in cooker and pour in water. Set custard cups on rack. Cover and set control at 5. Cook 1 minute after control jiggles. (For cookers having 15 pound setting only, remove from heat as soon as control jiggles.) Remove cooker from heat and reduce pressure normally. Refrigerate custards until time of feeding. Makes 2 custards.

*If glass or cermaic custard cups are used, increase cooking time to 2-1/2 minutes after control jiggles, for 5 pound setting. Cook 1 minute after control jiggles for cooker having 15 pound setting only.

As the infant nears the end of the first year, you may introduce some new flavors.

Vanilla Custard: Add a little pure vanilla extract.

Tapioca Custard: Add 1 tablespoon quick cooking tapioca to hot milk and follow basic recipe.

Chocolate Custard: Shave 1/2 square semi-sweet chocolate into hot milk and follow basic recipe. (Use only at 12 months or over.)

Banana Custard: Add 1 tablespoon mashed banana to hot milk and follow basic recipe.

Grape Nuts Custard: Add 1 tablespoon Grape Nuts to custard mixture. Stir to blend. (Use only after baby has some teeth and can chew.)

Soy Milk Custard: Follow basic recipe, substituting soy milk for pasteurized milk. I am including this for babies, or anyone, allergic to milk.

When adapting your own recipes for dishes that are to be cooked in a mold covered with foil be sure to increase cooking time a few minutes.

FRESH FRUITS FOR BABY

Fresh fruits cook quite quickly. Those showing 0 cooking time should be removed from heat as soon as control jiggles. Reduce pressure normally.

All fruit for strained baby food must be cooked, except banana.

Fruit	Cups of Water Per Pound	Pounds Pressure	Cooking Time After Control Jiggles
Apricots	1-1/2	5*	0
Apples	2	5*	0
Peaches	1-1/4	5*	0
Pears	1-1/4	5*	2 minutes
Plums, red or blue	1-1/4	5*	0

FRESH VEGETABLES FOR BABY

Follow directions given in Fresh Vegetables chart on page 121, but *increase* cooking time by 50 percent. Strain and serve. Prepare without salt.

*Timing is the same for cooker having 15 pound setting only.

172

CEREAL TABLE

Your pressure cooker will be a time and energy saver when you prepare long-cooking cereals. Measure water into cooker and bring to rapid boil. Add 1 tablespoon oil (check with pediatrician or nutritionist) to guard against frothing. Stir in cereal and bring to boil again. Reduce heat to medium for gas, to low for electric ranges. Cover and set control. Build up pressure slowly. Count cooking time when control beings to jiggle. Reduce pressure normally 5 minutes then place cooker under cold running water. To serve, you will have to add water, milk or formula after cooking is completed to make cereal the desired consistency. Do not add salt unless baby is on vegetarian diet.

Cereal	Cups Water 4 Quart Size	Cups Cereal Full Adult Strength	Pounds Pressure	Minutes to Cook After Control Jiggles
Corn Meal (Mix to a paste in 1 cup cold water. Add to boiling water.	1-3/4	1/2	15	10*
Hominy Grits	1-1/2	1/2	15	12 to 15*
Rolled Oats (Old Fashioned)	2	1/2	15	5*
Wheat Hearts	1	1/4	15	1*

*Reduce pressure normally 5 minutes, then place cooker under cold running water.

173

Tips For Dieters With Sodium, Fat And/Or Carbohydrate Restrictions

If you haven't used your pressure cooker for bonus results when sodium, fat and/or carbohydrates must be restricted, you have missed an opportunity to serve your dieter foods of improved flavor and texture and nutrient conservation. For this is just what your pressure cooker can accomplish. And in its use you will save time and money (by buying cheaper cuts of meat and other items) because with steam and fast cooking, you get all that a particular food has to yield.

For Sodium Control: Omit salt from all food to be cooked unless your diet list specifies the amount that may be used in daily cooking. Instead, sprinkle a salt substitute, if allowed, on dieter's portion at time of serving. Think flavors as you plan sodium restricted meals. Substitute a squeeze of lemon juice on vegetables, meat, salads and combination dishes for added zest to otherwise bland selections. Or use wine and herbs to spark your dishes.

If your dieter is severely restricted in sodium intake you may even have to count water used in food preparation. If sodium is less than 2.5 milligrams per cup, content may not be significant. In some parts of the country water contains as much as 5, 10 or even 15 milligrams sodium per cup and you'll have to count sodium in the water as part of free-choice items. Your pressure cooker can even help here too for you can place food on the rack to prevent it resting in water.

All restricted diets are individualized so follow your doctor's regimen.

Foods especially high in sodium are meat, fish, eggs, especially the white of egg, dark meat of poultry, milk, cream and cheese. In fact most food of animal origin is high in sodium as well as manufactured baked goods and specialties made with high sodium ingredients, such as the above listings plus baking powder, baking soda, salt and a whole parade of other commercially made products.

For sodium controlled diets, remember:

1. To eliminate any recipe in this book that contains non-allowed ingredients.
2. To get medical clearance of any ingredient in question.
3. To plan dieter's meals so adequate protein is assured.
4. To use only the kind of milk specified on diet list. Make no substitutions.
5. Not to overuse eggs, particularly egg white, because of high sodium content.
6. To skin poultry before browning as more sodium is in this part. Remember too that white meat of poultry has less sodium than dark.
7. That above all, your pressure cooker will do its best to give you maximum flavor whatever the restrictions are. Use flavorings and seasonings creatively

to spark otherwise bland dishes.

For Fat Control: The purpose of many fat controlled diets is to reduce weight and/or to reduce serum cholesterol levels. When there is too much cholesterol, a fatty substance in the blood, it may settle along arterial walls, thus narrowing the opening of the blood vessel so that the heart, brain or other organs may suffer or perish from lack of blood to these important areas of the body.

Consult your Heart Association for specific aids and research results. We know that the body manufactures cholesterol from some of the fats we eat. When a person develops arteriosclerosis it may be a sign that the body is getting too much fat as well as too much cholersterol.

Fats and oils contain a chemical element called *hydrogen*. If the fat or oil has all the hydrogen it can contain, it is called *saturated* fat. If it can take on more hydrogen, it is call an *unsaturated* fat . . . the more hydrogen it can absorb, the more unsaturated it becomes.

Usually the hardness of fat is a clue to its saturation. Foods that are usually solid at room temperature are generally highly saturated, such as meat and butter fats, egg yolk, most margarines, cheese and solid shortenings, among many. Fats that are liquid at room temperature . . . marine and vegetable oils . . . are highly unsaturated, except coconut and palm oils, which are highly saturated. Lowering cholesterol does seem to result in a lowering of serum cholesterol in many patients.

There also appears to be some connection between the amount of carbohydrate consumed and the level of serum triglycerides in some of the population. Carbohydrates are the sugars and starches in food. Some sugars come from ingredients, such as sugar, syrup, molasses, sweetened beverages, et. cetera. Some come from fruits, milk and other natural sugars. Starches are found in cereal grains and pastas, such as noodles, macaroni and like products. Starches are converted to sugar in the process of digestion. Very little sugar, as such is stored in the body. Most of it is converted into a substance called *triglyceride.*

When fat and carbohydrate must be controlled for health reasons, you can see the importance of following your doctor's directions with care.

For fat and/or carbohydrate diets, remember:

1. To prefer liquid fats to solid fats.
2. To reduce total fat content to allowable limit.
3. To select lean cuts of meat rather than fatter ones and to trim all meat of

visible fat before preparing.

4. That most luncheon meats are high in saturated fat and sodium.
5. That most commercially prepared foods contain more solid fat than home prepared ones.
6. To use only specified milk, such as nonfat or skim.
7. To aim to make the diet palatable to the patient and to provide adequate protein.
8. To use minimal amount of liquid oil in browning meats for dieter.
9. To remember that your pressure cooker can become your biggest aid in preparing nutritious and attractive looking and tasting controlled-fat dishes for your dieter. Your cooker can be a triple blessing providing good nutrition, saving you money, and conserving energy. Need I say more?

Recipes in this book were developed for a 4-quart cooker.

Index